1. Governmental Commissions on Green Taxes in Denmark

Jørgen Birk Mortensen and Jens Hauch

1.1 INTRODUCTION

Denmark has set relatively ambitious objectives for environmental protection. Economic instruments are increasingly applied in the process of achieving these objectives due to lack of cost-effectiveness in the traditional administrative environmental regulation.

High environmental standards are often assumed to decrease international competitiveness and reduce employment in a small open economy like Denmark's. This view has been very important in the Danish discussion and policy, but several attempts have also been made to estimate the cost or change in employment. Sometimes it is also argued in the discussion, that in a long term perspective high environmental standard and strict implementation can force domestic industries to innovate cleaner technologies and in this way improve international competitiveness, if world demand for these technologies expands in the future.

The macroeconomic effect of stricter environmental regulation simulated in the standard applied macroeconomic and general equilibrium simulation models used in Denmark seems to be rather small. The administrative costs associated with the use of environmental taxes have generally been low. Often the environmental taxes have been introduced on products already liable to charge of some form, so the environmental tax has been relatively inexpensive to administer.

1.2 TAX-REFORMS IN DENMARK

During the 1980s Denmark had a tax reform discussion like most of the countries in the OECD area. A major tax-reform cutting marginal taxes on personal income was approved in 1993. The Danish income tax reform is not

Green Taxes

as ambitious as the reforms in Norway and Sweden, but has the same characteristics: broader personal and corporate income tax base; a more consistent taxation of fringe benefits and capital gains; and elimination of a number of special deductions. Part of the loss of revenue is financed by increase in revenue from environmental taxes, as shown in Table 1.1.

Table 1.1   Financing the tax reform, billions of DKR

	1994	1995	1996	1997	1998
Loss of revenue:					
Lowering of personal income taxes	-20	-25.9	-31.8	-37.5	-45.9
Other measures	-1.1	-1.6	-1.7	-2	-2.1
Increase in revenue:					
Social security contributions	10.5	13.4	16.7	20.5	21.9
Environmental taxes	2.6	5.2	7.7	10	12.2
Broadening of the tax base	3.4	4.7	6.3	7.8	10.5
Other measures	-	-	-	0.8	2.8
Total loss of revenue	4.6	4.2	2.8	0.4	0.6

Source: Ministry of Finance.

The type and rate of increase in different environmental taxes are shown in Table 1.2.

The charge on gasoline is an energy tax but with a tax differentiation for unleaded gasoline. The charge on coal is a CO_2-tax.

1.3 GOVERNMENTAL COMMISSION ON PERSONAL INCOME (1992)

The tax reform was prepared by the work of a governmental commission on personal income. The commission wrote a chapter on green taxes and introduced the idea of using green taxes to reduce income taxes and 'the double dividend argument' in the Danish tax debate.

Table 1.2   Some environmental charges in the Danish 1994 tax reform

	1993	1994	1995	1996	1997	1998
Water consumption, DKK/m^3	0.46	0.51	0.54	0.58	0.63	0.71
Petroleum (leaded), DKK/litre	3.63	3.88	4.31	4.66	4.73	4.79
Petroleum (unleaded), DKK/litre	2.81	3.06	3.5	3.85	3.91	3.98
Shoping bags, DKK/item	-	0.63	0.63	0.63	0.63	0.63
Coal, DKK/ton	1165	1165	1265	1378	1490	1603
Waste disposal, DKK/ton	200	200	200	200	263	263

Source: Ministry of Taxation (1994).

There has been a broad interest in Denmark in the potential of environmental taxes to reduce overall costs in raising fiscal revenues. Do the revenues raised from new environmental taxes produce an additional benefit in the sense that they allow other taxes, which may have large distortionary effects on labour supply, investment or consumption, to be reduced?

The double dividend hypothesis (the weak form or the environmental view in Goulders (1994) terminology) claims that the tax revenues from green taxes can be used to reduce other distortionary taxes and hence improve the efficiency of the rest of the tax system. So green taxes will both improve the environment and reduce the distortions of the existing tax system. A positive environmental dividend from a green tax is that it is often taken for granted in the discussion, but there is an ongoing debate, also in Denmark, about the existence of the second dividend of the tax system (Andersen, 1995).

The first CO_2 in Denmark was introduced in 1992 and changed in 1995. Emissions of CO_2 are directly linked to fuel characteristics, so a tax differentiated on the basis of carbon content serves as a tax on CO_2-emissions. The tax rate applied to households deviates substantially from the tax rates applicable to industries or other commercial activities. Different tax levels and reduced rates for energy intensive firms are clearly inconsistent with economic efficiency.

From an economic point of view the 1994 CO_2-tax commission produced the most interesting report called 'Green taxes and enterprises'. The arguments from environmental economics for green taxes were discussed and possible conflict between international competitiveness and environmental regulation were clearly addressed. Different CO_2-tax model for minimizing the decrease in international competitiveness and employment were suggested.

The suggestions included recycling of CO_2-tax revenues to the business sector and fixed deductions in the CO_2-taxes to decrease profit loss, but still keeping the incentives right. The macroeconomic model used by the ministry of finance was used to estimate the consequences for different sectors and for employment. Unfortunately the final political decision did show that efficiency arguments were not important for the policy makers.

1.4 REGIONAL CONSEQUENCES OF A CO_2-TAX

Regional and distributional consequences of a CO_2-tax with a corresponding reduction in income tax base have been simulated by Mette Gertz using a regional model system for Denmark. Table 1.3 illustrates the regional differences. Regions with high income per head and an important service sector will experience gains and regions with low income per head and important primary production or traditional industries will experience a decrease in economic activity.

1.5 THE GESMEC MODEL[1]

The Secretariat of the Danish Economic Council has developed a CGE model, GESMEC (General Equilibrium Simulation Model of the Economic Council), of the Danish economy in order to calculate the long run costs for Denmark of various CO_2 reducing measures and Danish gains of international

---

1   This section is mainly based on Frandsen et al. (1995).

trade liberalizations scenarios, cf. Danish Economic Council (1993a), Danish Economic Council (1993b), Frandsen et al. (1994). In 1995 the model was further developed with refined dynamic properties and improved estimation of parameters, cf. Frandsen et al. (1995). In this chapter we will concentrate on the CO_2 aspects of the new version of the model.[2]

The present version of GESMEC includes 29 production sectors of which five are energy sectors and five are agricultural sectors. The sectors use as inputs one homogenous type of labour, one homogenous type of capital, 30 types of intermediate products either of domestic or foreign origin and one homogenous type of land (used only in the agricultural sectors). The model also includes 15 different types of consumer goods.

The model is mainly based on the theoretical structure of the Australian ORANI-F model, cf. Horridge et al. (1993). The behaviour of economic agents in GESMEC is modelled according to orthodox neoclassical microeconomic theory with relative prices playing a major role in the determination of economic outcomes. Producers minimize costs subject to a given production technology, and consumers maximize utility. The model assumes perfect competition in all markets, and domestic and foreign goods are treated as imperfect substitutes according to Armington's (1969) specification. Exports are determined by exogenous foreign demand and the relative Danish export price measured in foreign currency. It is assumed that labour and capital are perfect mobiles between industries. Total public consumption is exogenous and there is no explicit sector budget constraint.

Focusing on sectoral production, each sector produces under constant returns to scale. Given sectoral demand and relative prices, producers minimize costs by using optimal quantities of intermediate inputs and an aggregate of energy, labour, capital and agricultural land. In Figure 1.1, the overall production structure of the model is represented by a tree. On the first level the optimal combination of special imports, taxes and the aggregate of capital, land, labour, intermediate allocation procedures substitution possibilities are allowed by using CES functions. The next level determines how energy, capital, land and labour are substituting intermediate inputs and so on. The bottom level determines, by the Armington specification, the producers demand for foreign and domestic commodities.

A single representative consumer is assumed to buy 15 different groups of consumer goods. There is no aggregate consumption function in the model, as the total real private consumption is determined implicitly by an exogenous balance of goods and services in the standard closure. Given total expenditure on consumer goods and assuming different expenditure elasticities of

---

2   The opinions expressed by the authors are not necessarily shared by the Chairmanship of the Danish Economic Council.

Table 1.3   Change in the value of production and employment

Region	Change in production, %	Change in employment (Number of people)
Copenhagen	0.02	190
West Zealand County	-0.01	10
Storströms County	0.01	20
Bornholm County	-0.05	-10
Funen County	0.02	40
Southern Jutland County	-	10
Ribe County	-0.06	-20
Vejle County	-0.01	0
Ringköbing County	-0.03	-20
Århus County	0.01	40
Viborg County	-0.02	0
Northern Jutland	-0.01	0
Entire country	0.00	270

Source: Mette Görtz. (It is assumed that the reduction in income taxes will slow down the rate of wage increases).

demand, consumers decide how much to spend in each group depending on relative prices. Finally, consumers decide, for each of these goods the import share subject to relative prices and the elasticity of substitution between goods from the two types of origin.

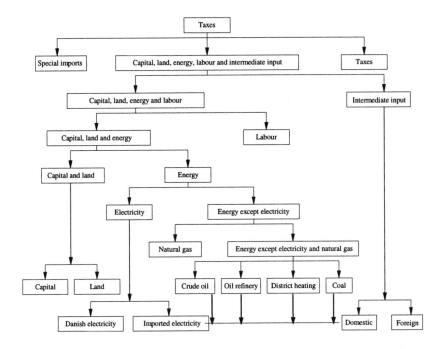

Figure 1.1   Overall production structure

A submodel determines the energy related CO_2 emission from the base year CO_2 emission matrix. The base year emission matrix is compiled by multiplying the detailed Danish energy matrices relating the gross use of 25 fuels at basic value to economic activity, cf. Denmark Statistics (1993). Finally, the emission matrix is aggregated to the level of aggregation of the main model.

1.6 GESMEC RESULTS

It is an official Danish policy target to reduce Danish CO_2 emissions by 20 per cent by the year 2005 relative to the level of emissions in 1988. However, in the absence of specific CO_2 emission reducing measures it was officially estimated in 1990 that emissions would increase by 5 per cent during that period. Specific emission reducing measures should therefore generate a total reduction of approximately 25 per cent by 2005. The results of the scenarios that will be presented below are reported in Appendix 1.

1.6.1   Scenario 1: Use of Economic Regulative Instruments

In this scenario we present the consequences of an isolated Danish reduction in the CO_2 discharge by 25 per cent. The instrument is a tax on total Danish energy use in households and industries. It is assumed that households and industries can react on the tax without adjustment costs. To ensure that this tax should be announced and gradually implemented it is further assumed that all markets are clear due to totally flexible prices and wages. The tax is the same in all sectors but is differentiated by the content of CO_2 in fuels. This means that coal is taxed more heavily than oil which is taxed more heavily than natural gas. The tax is primarily on raw energy products, and the energy converting sectors can respond to the tax by changing their input structure. The tax revenue is 13 billion of DKK (approximately equal to 2.4 billion of USD) which corresponds to a tax of 300 DKK per ton CO_2. The fiscal policy is implicitly assumed to be adjusted to ensure that the current account is not affected. The calculations show that private consumption is 0.3 per cent lower and GDP 0.7 per cent lower, cf. Appendix 1. The costs are small but significant. Denmark contributes to the global discharge of CO_2 by 0.3-0.4 per cent so the global level of CO_2 discharge will be almost unaffected by Denmark introducing CO_2 taxes.

The calculations do not account for the possibility of receiving double dividends when using the CO_2 tax revenue to reduce income tax. The consequences for industrial production, employment, operating surplus and final prices are reported in Appendix 2. The industries are affected differently depending on differences in their energy intensity and their possibilities of increasing their final prices (their exposure to competition). This is one reason that production in 'other services' is almost unaffected, while the production in 'construction suppliers' is reduced by 4.6 per cent. Both industries are primarily producing for the domestic market, but 'construction suppliers' have a significantly higher energy intensity than 'other services'.

1.6.2   Scenario 2: Adjustment Costs

If the period is shorter than the 15 years used in Scenario 1 (1990-2005), industries and households might face significant costs of adjusting to the CO_2 tax. These costs will be analyzed in Scenario 2. The horizon is eight years (1990-98), and the target is a 25 per cent reduction of the Danish CO_2 discharge. The industries' and households' possibilities of substituting energy with other inputs are limited compared to Scenario 1 in which there were no adjustment costs. Technically, it is assumed that the industries' elasticity of substitution is scaled down from 0.3 to 0.15. The price elasticity that describes the households' demand for energy is similarly assumed to be halved. It is, moreover, assumed that nominal wages are inflexible.

With those assumptions private consumption is lowered by 1.1 per cent, which is four times as much as in Scenario 1. The necessary tax is 700 DKK per ton of CO_2, which is higher than in Scenario 1 because the industries have less possibilities of substitution. The competitiveness is lowered by 1.8 per cent, which is three times as much as in Scenario 1. One of the reasons for this is the inflexible labour market that does not, like in Scenario 1, cushion the loss of competitiveness by lower wages. The result is a reduction in employment of 3.4 per cent corresponding to 90 000 persons.

This scenario illustrates that the social costs of the environment and energy policies can be increased dramatically if the target is carried through without any attention to the costs of adjustment in the labour market and in industries and households.

1.6.3   Scenario 3: Costs of Using Administrative Instruments

Economic theory will generally predict that economic instruments are more effective than administrative instruments, as it is more efficient to combat pollution in the cheapest way, cf. Danish Economic Council (1995), in this scenario the possible economic consequences of using administrative v. economic instruments are analyzed. The economic instrument is the tax used in Scenario 1, while the administrative instrument forces the energy converting industries to reduce all their energy inputs by 25 per cent. The reductions are carried through without any attention to how it could be done more cheaply. In the Danish energy and environmental policy, administrative instruments are not used as described here, and the comparison of the two instruments are only able to show the maximal loss of welfare.

If quotas are imposed on the inputs in the energy converting industries, the supply of energy will be smaller, which implies that the prices paid by households and industries will be increased which again implies lower demand. The possibility of foreign exporters of energy using the situation to increase their prices is deciding what the consequences of this type of regulation will be. It is necessary to distinguish between exporters of primary energy products (crude oil and coal) that primarily sell their products to the energy converting sectors, and manufactured energy to Denmark (primarily refined oil) that is sold to industries and manufactured energy to Denmark (primarily refined oil) that is sold to industries and households. The fact that the world market for crude oil and coal is characterized by almost perfect competition means that the exporters of those energy products are not expected to be able to increase the price when they are selling to the Danish energy converting industries. The situation is different when it comes to foreign converted energy (refined oil) in Denmark, as the distribution is partly monopolized and mainly privately owned. There is a large risk that the extra profits from the increased prices will go to the foreign distributers.

It also assumed in this scenario that the import price of refined oil is following the Danish refineries selling price and that the foreign energy producers receive extra profits. The effect is an increase in the total import price of 4.5 per cent. Real wages are lowered by 5 per cent as a result of 1.6 per cent higher retail prices, and 3.4 per cent lower nominal wages. Private consumption is 2.8 per cent lower, which is 9-10 times as much as in Scenario 1 in which the economic instrument was used.

If the import prices of refined oil do not change, the effect on private consumption will be only 0.7 per cent (this scenario is not reported in Appendix 1), primarily stemming from the lost cost efficiency. This implies that the decrease of private consumption is only 2-3 times higher than it was with the economic instruments. It is interesting that it is primarily the effect on the terms of trade that is lowering private consumption, while the loss of cost efficiency is only lowering the private consumption by 0.7 per cent.

APPENDIX 1: EFFECTS OF A CO_2 REDUCTION AT 25 PER CENT OBTAINED BY DIFFERENT INSTRUMENTS

	Scenario 1	Scenario 2	Scenario 3
Changes in per cent:			
Real GDP	-0.7	-3.9	-1.5
Investment	-0.3	-1.1	-2.8
Export volume	-2.2	-17.4	-7.1
Import volume	-2.5	-7.1	-5.3
Aggregate capital stock	-0.6	-3.5	-1.9
Export prices	0.6	1.8	0.1
Import prices	0	0	4.4
Terms of trade	0.6	1.8	-4.3
Capital rental prices	0.4	1.2	-1.4
Consumer prices	3.2	8.6	1.6
Nominal wage	-0.6	0	-3.4
Employment	0	-3.4	0
Global CO_2 discharge	-0.1	-0.1	-0.1
Danish CO_2 discharge	-25.0	-25.0	-25.0
Absolute changes:			
Balance on goods and services, billion DKK	0	0	0
Tax revenue, billion DKK	13.3	31.1	-
Exogenous changes:			
Tax on raw coal	59.6	144.8	
Tax on raw oil	96.4	234.7	
Tax on refined oil	82.8	201.8	
Tax on electricity	51.8	125.8	
Tax on district heating	17.3	42.2	
Tax on coal	271.5	659.2	

REFERENCES

Andersen, T.M. (1995), 'Miljöprojekter fra et makroperspektiv' in C. Hjort-Andersen (ed.), *Ökonomisk vurdering av energiprojekter*, Copenhagen.

Andersen, F.M., Kilde, N.A., Nielsen, L.H. and Praestgård, S. (1991), 'En teknisk-ekonomisk prognosemodel for industriens energiforbrug samt energirelaterede CO_2-, SO_2- of NO_x-emissioner', *INDUS-Version 2, EMIS.* Forskningscenter RISÖ, Roskilde.

Armington, P.S. (1969), 'A theory of demand for products distinguished by place of production', *IMF Staff Papers* **26**, Washington.

Danish Economic Council (1993a), *Danish Economy,* May 1993, Copenhagen.

Danish Economic Council (1993b), *Danish Economy,* November 1993, Copenhagen.

Danish Economic Council (1995), *Danish Economy,* Spring 1995, Copenhagen.

Frandsen, S.E., Hansen, J.V. and Trier, P. (1994), 'A general equilibrium model for Denmark with two applications', *Economic & Financial Modeling,* Summer 1994.

Frandsen, S.E., Hansen, J.V. and Trier, P. (1995), 'GESMEC En generel ligevaegtsmodel for Denmark', *Dokumentation og Anvendelser,* Copenhagen.

Görtz, M. (1995), 'Regional consequences of environmental taxes', in J.B. Mortensen, A.-M.B. Christensen, C. Jensen-Butler and B. Madsen (eds), *Modelling the Economy and the Environment,* Springer Verlag.

Horridge, J.M., Parmenter, B.R. and Pearson, K.R. (1993), 'ORANI-F: A general equilibirum model of the Australian economy', *Economic and Financial Computering,* Summer 1993.

2. The Governmental Commission on Green Taxes in Norway

Vidar Christiansen and Ing-Marie Gren

2.1 INTRODUCTION

The Norwegian Green Tax Commission was appointed by the government in December 1994 subsequent to a parliamentary initiative. It started work early in 1995. The deadline for presenting its report was May 1996. The Commission has 116 members from ministries (Finance, Environment, Transport, Energy etc.), academic and other research institutions and interest groups (environmental organizations, the main association of trade unions, the manufacturing and oil industry). There are no political members. According to the mandate *the main task is to examine revenue neutral tax reforms for the purpose of achieving higher employment and a better environment.*

In particular the Commission is asked to consider how these goals can be attained by shifting taxes from labour to activities using natural resources and harming the environment. Both short and long term effects should be explored, but sustainable development and high employment in a long term perspective are emphasized. It is part of the task to provide empirical studies of how various industries will be affected. The Commission is asked to take into account considerations that may not be easily reconciled. It is desirable that Norway should play a pioneering role among countries in environmental policy. On the other hand the position of Norway as a large producer and exporter of energy should be observed. The Commission is asked to report on relevant studies from other countries and international organizations. It is also asked to report on the tax and environmental policy adopted in other countries. Finally, the Commission is requested to examine distributional effects and transitional problems generated by its proposed tax reforms.

The Commission used work done in various countries and institutions, but also initiated a number of studies which were regarded as useful inputs in the work of the Commission. These cover facts, theoretical and empirical issues. The studies were done by ministries, the secretariat or member of the

Commission and persons outside the Commission. These studies can be divided into two classes:

(i)   Surveys of major environmental problems, present tax systems in Norway and internationally, unemployment and the Norwegian energy exports;

(ii) Partial analyses of impacts of taxes on pollutant emissions, rents from use of natural resources, and changes in environmentally harmful subsidies.

The objectives with these studies are to establish certain data, to create a conceptual and theoretical framework for discussing socially desirable tax reforms, and to examine empirical implications of making taxes greener. The approach is to combine scenarios from macroeconomic models with micro oriented sector studies. There is particular interest in sectors that are potentially large loosers or gainers from such tax reforms. Characteristics like the scope for factor substitution, employment, pollution, international competition, etc., are described. There is also interest in sectors generating a pure rent that may be a base for non distortionary taxes. (Some of these sectors have been addressed separately in other contexts, and were not dealt with by the Commission)

Based on the results from these partial studies, the Commission identified proposals for reform which can be implemented in the short run and measures which need further investigation. In the following the partial studies are briefly presented. The section ends with a presentation of the Commission proposals.

2.2 SURVEYS OF NORWEGIAN CURRENT ENVIRONMENTAL PROBLEMS, TAX SYSTEM, UNEMPLOYMENT AND ENERGY PRODUCTION

One component of the main objective of the Commission's task is to identify taxes which are environmentally improving. It is then necessary to have some knowledge of the environmental conditions and harmful activities. In a small country like Norway, a considerable part of the sources of several environmental problems, such as climate change and acidification, are found outside the Norwegian borders. In a similar way, the environmental impacts of Norwegian reductions in emissions occur in other countries. The Commission does not, however, try to relate emission reductions to environmental impacts. Instead, an investigation of different important emissions is carried out together with a list of current Norwegian environmental problems.

The environmental emissions and problems have been of political concern for a period of about 25 years, and therefore several types of environmental taxes have already been introduced. Highly related to pollutant emissions is the energy sector and, in particular, petroleum production and exports. Therefore, special concern is given to the role of the petroleum producing sector and energy intensive manufacturing in an ecological tax reform.

2.2.1 Current environmental problems

Norway, like all other countries is concerned with the climate changes caused by emissions of carbon dioxides and other pollutants. Current (1995) emissions amount to 37.7 millions of CO_2, which corresponds to about 2 per millage of total global emissions. About 80 per cent of emissions originate respectively from mobile and stationary combustion sources. It is expected that Norwegian emissions will increase by about 18 per cent by 2010 due to increased traffic.

In spite of the relatively large natural areas in Norway, another environmental problem of great concern are reductions in biodiversity. It is estimated that 40 000 different species exist in Norway. Only enough is known about a quarter of these to draw any conclusions about threats to their extinction. About 15 per cent are under direct threat from extinction. Of commercial interest is the reduction in certain fish species. The major impact on the composition of species in inland water is acid pollution, of which 10 per cent originates from Norwegian sources (sulphur and nitrogen dioxides). Currently, the deposition exceeds critical loads in more than one third of Norway. An improvement is expected from the 1994 international sulphur.

Other internationally related environmental problems in Norway are damage from ground layer ozone and local problems from air pollution in certain environmentally sensitive areas. It is expected that these and the above mentioned problems are very much related to the environmental policies in other European countries.

Of more national origin are environmental problems associated with waste and eutrophication. In total, 5 million tons of waste are produced every year exclusive of building material and mining waste. About 650 000 tons are regarded as especially environmentally damaging, mainly by destroying water quality, generating the climate gas methane, and contributing to eutrophication. About 12 per cent of the waste is currently reused. It is expected that within a few years, there will be no untreated waste in Norway. Households and agriculture also contribute to damage from eutrophication by emissions of nutrients: nitrogen and phosphorus. Norway, like many other countries faces problems with implementing instruments for reducing emissions from the agricultural sector.

2.2.2   Current tax system

During 1965-80, the total taxes as related to GDP increased from about 32 per cent to about 47 per cent. In 1995, total taxes were reduced to 40.8 per cent of GDP. Taxes on labour income is the dominating source of tax incomes. The tax wedge in Norway is lower than in several European OECD countries and corresponds to 60 per cent (in 1991-2). It is recognized that a source of inefficiency in the tax system is the unequal treatment of different incomes from capital. On the other hand, this tax base accounts for only about 15 per cent of total tax revenue.

The Commission recognizes that the environmentally related fiscal policies are, in an international perspective, relatively high in Norway. This can be regarded as a reflection of the environmental concerns nationally and internationally. The most serious international environmental problems are associated with global climatic change. Norway is one of the five countries that has introduced charges (the others are Denmark, Finland, Netherlands, and Sweden), and is leading with a level of CO_2 charge on gasoline. In addition to these charges, Norway also introduced charges on, among other things, other petroleum products, fertilizers, sulphur, and pesticides. In total, environmentally related charges in Norway account for about 15 per cent of total fiscal income. The composition of different environmental charges and taxes is presented in Table 2.1.

The largest source of fiscal income is taxes on rents and incomes from petroleum products. The second source is different taxes on vehicles: purchase taxes, annual charges, weightrelated charges, and re-registration charges.

2.2.3   Unemployment

In Norway, like many other countries, the level of unemployment as a fraction of the total labour force has increased during the last 15 years. During 1980 the unemployment rate was 2 per cent which increased and peaked at 6 per cent in 1993, and then decreased to 4.4 per cent in 1996. Although these are relatively low rates as compared to most other OECD countries, current rates of long term unemployment are high by previous standards in Norway. According to macro economic forecasts, the unemployment rate will decline to 3.5 per cent within a few years. The Commission points at the optimistic scenarios in the model with respect to international competition, which will imply a higher rate of unemployment. It is also emphasized, that even if the forecasts are fulfilled, it will be difficult for labour with a low education and young people with little experience to find a job. Therefore, a labour policy with special focus on these exposed groups will be necessary in the future.

Green Taxes

NEW HORIZONS IN ENVIRONMENTAL ECONOMICS

General Editors: Wallace E. Oates, *Professor of Economics, University of Maryland, USA* and Henk Folmer, *Professor of Economics, Wageningen Agricultural University, The Netherlands and Professor of Environmental Economics, Tilburg University, The Netherlands*

This important series is designed to make a significant contribution to the development of the principles and practices of environmental economics. It includes both theoretical and empirical work. International in scope, it addresses issues of current and future concern in both East and West and in developed and developing countries.

The main purpose of the series is to create a forum for the publication of high quality work and to show how economic analysis can make a contribution to understanding and resolving the environmental problems confronting the world in the late twentieth century.

Recent titles in the series include:

Environmental Transition in Nordic and Baltic Countries
Edited by Hans Aage

Biodiversity, Conservation and Sustainable Development
Principles and Practices with Asian Examples
Clem Tisdell

Green Taxes
Economic Theory and Empirical Evidence from Scandinavia
Edited by Runar Brännlund and Ing-Marie Gren

The Political Economy of Environmental Policy
A Public Choice Approach to Market Instruments
Bouwe R. Dijkstra

The Economic Valuation of Landscape Change
Theory and Policies for Land Use and Conservation
José Manuel L. Santos

Sustaining Development
Environmental Resources in Developing Countries
Daniel W. Bromley

Valuing Recreation and the Environment
Revealed Preference Methods in Theory and Practice
Edited by Joseph A. Herriges and Catherine L. Kling

Designing Effective Environmental Regimes
The Key Conditions
Jørgen Wettestad

Environmental Networks
A Framework for Economic Decision-Making and Policy Analysis
Kanwalroop Kathy Dhanda, Anna Nagurney and Padma Ramanujam

The International Yearbook of Environmental and Resource Economics
1999/2000
Edited by Henk Folmer and Tom Tietenberg

Green Taxes

Economic Theory and Empirical Evidence from Scandinavia

Edited by

Runar Brännlund

Department of Economics, Umeå University, Sweden

and

Ing-Marie Gren

Department of Economics, The Swedish University of Agricultural Sciences, Uppsala, Sweden

NEW HORIZONS IN ENVIRONMENTAL ECONOMICS

Edward Elgar
Cheltenham, UK • Northampton, MA, USA

Published by
Edward Elgar Publishing Limited
Glensanda House
Montpellier Parade
Cheltenham
Glos GL50 1UA
UK

Edward Elgar Publishing, Inc.
6 Market Street
Northampton
Massachusetts 01060
USA

A catalogue record for this book
is available from the British Library

Library of Congress Cataloguing in Publication Data

Green taxes: economic theory and empirical evidence from Scandinavia
/ edited by Runar Brännlund, Ing-Marie Gren.
    (New horizons in environmental economics series)
    Based on a Nordic workshop held in Stockholm, 1995.
    Includes bibliographical references.
    1. Environmental impact charges—Scandinavia—Congresses.
I. Brännlund, R. (Runar) II. Gren, Ing-Marie. III. Series: New
horizons in environmental economics.
HJ5429.95.G74 1999
336.2—dc21
                                        98–46609
                                           CIP

ISBN 1 85898 859 4
Printed and bound in Great Britain by
MPG Books Ltd, Bodmin, Cornwall

Contents

List of Figures

List of Tables

Introduction

Runar Brännlund and Ing-Marie Gren

In spring 1995 the Swedish Green Tax Commission was appointed by the Swedish government. From a Swedish perspective it is possible to identify two main reasons for appointing this committee. First of all, there has been a growing interest, and concern, about environmental problems for quite a long time in Sweden. In addition it has been discovered, on the political scene, that economic instruments, such as taxes, may be an efficient weapon in the battle against environmental problems. Thus, it became apparent that not only would environmental taxes bring us healthy tax revenues in a time of heavy budget deficits, it would also, at the same time, give an improved environmental quality. Secondly, the increasing unemployment rate in Sweden during the 1990s has been a very disturbing development in light of the Swedish tradition of keeping unemployment at minimum levels by all means. The main reason for the increase in unemployment can, of course, be found in economic recession during the last years. However, another explanation, among others, to this disturbing development was that high income and labour taxes have created inefficient resource allocation in general, and inefficiencies in labour participation rates in particular. It was in the light of this that the Green Tax Commission was born. The question that was posed was: would it be possible to improve environmental quality and as a second dividend get an efficiency improvement in resource allocation, which would lead to a reduction in unemployment? The simple, and very sound, idea was to use taxes to adjust prices for various resources. In other words, we should tax 'good' things, such as labour, to a lesser extent, and 'bad' things, such as pollution, to a larger extent.

This basic question has been raised by, among others, Oates (1991) and Pearce (1991) who viewed such a tax swap as a promising device for solving the two problems of bad environment and a high level of unemployment. However, later theoretical work has been more hesitant on the potential of a 'free lunch' by pointing at the general equilibrium effects caused by changes in the relative prices of inputs and outputs associated by a tax swap (e.g. Bovenberg and De Mooij 1994, Bovenberg and van der Ploeg 1994, Goulder 1995, and Bovenberg and Goulder 1996). In this spirit, enthusiasm mixed with some hesitation, the Swedish Commission as well as governmental commissions in several other European countries were started up.

In this volume we concentrate on the potential of ecological tax reforms in the Nordic countries, especially in Sweden. The main reasons are the relatively long term environmental concerns in these countries, which have resulted in environmental taxes on several environmentally damaging activities. Another factor is the importance of international competitiveness for these countries. The countries have also shared the experiences of relatively high levels of unemployment and budget deficits. With this background it is of interest to investigate the issues of an ecological tax reform brought up by the country governmental commissions and to compare them with the main findings from economic theory and empirical applications. In this setting, the volume can be regarded as complementary to another volume on ecological tax reforms, Carraro and Siniscalco (1996), in two respects: the inclusion of actual governmental commissions, and the empirical results mainly from Sweden with brief report results in Denmark and Norway. The main questions addressed here can then be stated as follows

- What are the concerns of the commissions on green taxes in the different Nordic countries?
- What do we know from economic theory on the existence of 'double' or more dividends?
- What are the results from empirical research?

The main part of this volume is the result of a Nordic workshop in September 1995 at the Beijer Institute of Ecological Economics in Stockholm. The workshop was organized jointly by the Swedish Commission on Green Taxes and Beijer International Institute of Ecological Economics. The purpose was to share experiences and interests on ecological tax reforms among the Nordic countries on the above three issues.

In this volume the chapters are presented in accordance with the above three questions. The first three chapters concern commissions on green taxes from three Nordic countries: Denmark, Norway and Sweden. Common to all three governmental commissions is the concern of four interrelated issues: environment, unemployment, fiscal revenues and international competitiveness. All commissions were also simulating costs of CO_2 charges by means of computable equilibrium models. The Swedish model is presented in the Chapters 6, 7 and 8. Both the Norwegian and the Swedish commissions also carried out partial analysis of the labour market, especially the labour supply, and investigations of important sectors.

Chapter 4 of this volume contains theoretical discussion on the existence of the double dividend, i.e. that the introduction or increase in environmental taxes combined with revenue neutral reduction in labour taxes has a positive impact on employment and welfare disregarding the environmental benefits. In Chapter 4 David Starrett sorts out the different concepts of double dividend which have been used in the literature. By means of a simple model in which there are only two goods which are taxed initially, a clean and a dirty good, he argues that there are some presumptions of the existence of a weak positive double dividend, i.e. there is some scope for extra benefits of an environmental tax given a specific value of the marginal social damage from pollution. A strong double dividend implies that there is some extra benefit no matter how small the environmental effect is. Starrett is less optimistic about this occurrence since it requires that demand for the clean good would have to be relatively more elastic than that for the dirty good. Starrett continues to discuss the case when labour is also the subject to preexisting taxes. In this case he is rather pessimistic about the likelihood of a double dividend. The reason for this pessimistic view is that under normal conditions leisure and other goods are substitutes. A tax swap under these circumstances would give rise to two effects: a revenue recycling effect, which is positive since a reduction of the labour tax reduces distortions in terms of more employment, and a tax interaction effect, which is negative since a higher consumer price on goods increases demand for leisure, since leisure and goods are substitutes. An increase in leisure means less labour, which in turn means less labour tax revenues. Starrett concludes that the negative tax interaction effect dominates for a 'neutral' specification of parameters.

Chapters 5, 6, 7 and 8 present representative empirical analyses connected to ecological tax reform. One is the social costs associated with the introduction and/or increases of environmentally related taxes. Goulder's and the Harrison and Kriström chapters present such cost estimates using numerical general equilibrium models. Another issue concerns the effects on energy demand in various sectors and the effects on the labour market from changes in energy and labour taxes. Brännlund and Gren make use of an econometric partial equilibrium model to estimate demand elasticities for various energy goods in Sweden. Magnus Wikström makes a summary of Swedish experiences from estimating the labour supply curve by the application of meta analysis.

Lawrence Goulder's contribution in Chapter 5 can be regarded as a link between the theoretical issues discussed in Starrett's paper and the empirical applications. He starts with a brief review of current theoretical concerns from which he discusses empirical need. Results from a dynamic computable equilibrium model of the US economy are presented. He notices the general theoretical agreement on the net gains from redistributing emission taxes by reducing other distorting taxes instead of returning them as a lump sum. When the marginal excess burden of taxes between different products differs there is a potential for a positive double dividend if the burden of the emissions taxes falls on the factor with relatively low marginal excess burden. Calculations from the US economy show that the marginal excess burden of taxes on capital is 0.43 and that of labour is 0.31. Thus, there should be a potential for a positive double dividend. The results from a numerical general equilibrium model also verify this. They indicate that the cost of taxes decreases considerably when the tax revenues from eight different emission taxes are used to decrease other taxes instead of returning them in a lump sum fashion. In other words, the results support the notion of a weak double dividend. The results, however, do not support the strong double dividend hypothesis, i.e., the simulated tax shift gives rise to an overall welfare cost, environmental benefits excluded.

In a similar fashion, impacts of a Swedish carbon tax are calculated by means of a static numerical general equilibrium model by Glenn Harrison and Bengt Kriström in Chapter 6. The specific Swedish conditions are taken into account in the construction of the model. These conditions include the relatively high environmental and energy taxes, the concern for international competitiveness, the referendum on abolishing nuclear power before the year 2010, freezing of carbon emissions at the level of 1990, and the recent membership of the European Union. In addition an attempt is made to include environmental benefits from carbon emission reductions, measured in monetary terms. According to the results, there is only a 'modest' aggregate decrease of Swedish carbon emissions due to a doubling of the Swedish carbon tax. The reason is that the adjustments within the economy not only reduce production in those sectors which are relatively carbon intensive, but also expand other sectors with less, but still positive, carbon emissions. The results also point to the tax interaction effects that may occur in a scenario where the CO_2 tax is increased. For example, an increase in the CO_2 tax on fossil fuels will reduce the tax revenues from the preexisting energy tax. The imposition of constraints on nuclear generation of electricity reduces carbon emissions due to the decline in energy production from increases in energy prices. Another thought-provoking result is the distributional impacts which indicate that the tax burdens are largest for families with many children. The inclusion of the environmental benefits estimate shows that a higher CO_2 tax can hardly be justified on cost benefit grounds.

Chapter 7 by Runar Brännlund and Ing-Marie Gren departs from the belief that is of great importance in the discussion of a green tax reform that it is necessary to have, at least a crude estimate of what the impact of individual taxes might be. Specifically there are two different, but related, impacts which are considered. The first one is the environmental effects from green taxes. The second one is the fiscal effects of green taxes. In contrast to the contributions by Goulder and by Harrison and Kriström the analysis completely ignores the general equilibrium effects. Instead a partial equilibrium view is taken where all agents are assumed to be price takers. The basic idea is to use econometric techniques to estimate demand elasticities for various energy goods. A high demand elasticity means in principle that a tax increase has a relatively large environmental effect, but also a substantial tax erosion effect. In order to analyse the sensitivity to price changes a partial equilibrium framework is employed. In this case this means an analysis of the industry, the household sector, and the agriculture sector separately. The taxes analysed are the CO_2 tax and the tax on nitrogen in fertilizers. The results from the analyses show that a higher CO_2 tax, and hence higher consumer price of fossil fuels, reduces demand for fossil fuels. The magnitude of the effects, however, is small. The same conclusion holds true concerning nitrogen demand in agriculture.

The last chapter by Magnus Wikström raises another difficult issue: the reactions on the labour market from changes in wages. This issue is approached by a meta analysis where the results of wage elasticities and income elasticities from a number of different Swedish studies are compared. These studies support the hypothesis of a positively sloped labour supply curve. Female labour supply seems to be more elastic than male supply. There is also a tendency towards a negative income elasticity. However, there is a great difference in quantitative results between the studies. Wikström tries to explain this by a number of different dummy variables. It turns out that sample selection and data sets mainly explain the difference between the studies.

When comparing the issues raised by the governmental commissions we note that neither the authors of the theoretical nor the authors of the empirical chapters simultaneously considered all four issues raised by the commissions. In spite of this, a common agreement is the probable non existence of a 'free lunch', i.e. that the level of unemployment can be decreased by revenue neutral environmental taxes without any costs to society disregarding the environmental benefits. This is one reason for the careful and modest recommendations made by the commissions. Further understanding of the functioning of the labour market, household decisions on leisure and other goods, and the link between changes in pollutant emissions and environmental damages as measured in monetary terms is needed in order to make more concrete suggestions concerning ecological tax reforms.

REFERENCES

Bovenberg, L. and Goulder, L. (1996), 'Optimal Environmental Taxation in the Presence of Other Taxes: General Equilibrium Analyses', *American Economic Review,* **86** (4), 985-1000.

Bovenberg, L. and De Mooij, R.A. (1994), 'Environmental Levies and Distortionary Taxation', *American Economic Review,* **84** (4), 1085-89.

Bovenberg, L. and van der Ploeg, F. (1994), 'Environmental Policy, Public Finance and the Labor Market in a Second-Best World', *Journal of Public Economics,* **55** (3), 349-90.

Carraro, C. and Siniscalco, D. (1996). *Environmental Fiscal Reform and Unemployment,* Dordrecht, Netherlands: Kluwer Academic Publishers.

Goulder, L.H. (1995), 'Effects of Carbon Taxes in an Economy with Prior Tax Distortions: An Intertemporal General Equilibrium Analysis', *Journal of Environmental Economics and Management*, **29** (3), 271-97.

Oates, W. (1991), *Pollution Charges as a Source of Public Revenues,* Washington, DC: Resources for the Future, Discussion paper, pp. 92-105.

Pearce, D. (1991), 'The role of carbon taxes in adjusting to global warming', *The Economic Journal* **101**, pp. 938-48.

Table 2.1   Incomes from environmentally related charges in 1995,
millions of NOK

Gasoline	9 941
Diesel	2 706
Mineral oil	1 400
CO_2	2 559
Oil production and incomes	16 682
Electricity production and consumption	4 409
Car	12 193
Air traffic	421
Boat engines	57
Packages	208
Lubricating oil	
Fertilizer	167
Pesticides	19
Total	50 822
% of fiscal budget	14
% of GDP	6

Source: NOU 1996.

2.2.4   Norway as a producer and exporter of energy

Of course, there are several relations between Norway's role as producer and
exporter of energy and her environmental and employment challenges.
Although Norway is the world's second largest exporter of oil products, she
accounts for about 4 per cent of the total output of energy in the world. The
impact on world market prices should therefore be negligible. Another
important reason for the small impact on demand for oil products is that in
most countries to which Norway exports, the charges account for more than
50 per cent of the consumer price. The charge is smaller on gas, which would
imply a higher impact on demand from Norwegian production decisions, on
the other hand, increases in consumer charges on oil products will have an
impact on Norwegian exports. According to model simulation results, a
global charge on CO_2 amounting to 360 NOK/tons may result in a decrease
in petroleum income by about 20 per cent. Under inefficient carbon
reductions, the losses will be higher. This illustrates a potential conflict
between the two goals of environmental and economic objectives There are

several uncertainties related to this issue such as forecasts of exports of gas and electricity from water power. Although the energy production has been important for creating employment opportunities in the past, these sectors are, in a macro perspective, of minor importance. Instead, generated fiscal revenue provides opportunities for an active employment policy.

2.3 PARTIAL ANALYSES OF ENVIRONMENTAL TAXES

Parallel to the inventory of Norwegian current tax and charge systems, work on analysis of principles of taxation in general and with environmental concerns was carried out. Two options for increasing budget incomes from taxes on environmentally degrading activities are identified: raise or introduce environmental tax and reduce subsidies generating environmental damage. Based on economic theory, the Norwegian Green Tax Commission identifies three basic principles for environmental taxation;

(1) The most desirable taxes are those improving the overall efficiency, such as taxes correcting environmental damage.
(2) The second best option is to use neutral taxes, which do not distort prices of goods, such as taxes on rent from fish and other natural resources.
(3) If these two options are not available or if these taxes do not give enough fiscal revenue, identify taxes which cause as little inefficiency as possible.

It is further noted that, in general, taxes on a large variety of factors or commodities are preferred to higher tax levels on a few factors. The reason is the smaller distortions, less adjustment by economic agents, caused by general taxes. The impacts of recycled environmental taxes on employment and unemployment are not clear. It seems, however, that decreases in income tax on labour, implies an increase in labour supply, and, in the long run, the level of employment. The relation between taxes and unemployment is much more uncertain. Theory does not offer any clear conclusions, and the results of empirical studies are ambiguous. Studies carried out within the Commission framework indicate a decrease in unemployment from a decrease in the payroll tax.

Computable equilibrium models are used in order to identify the mechanisms which determine the existence and magnitude of 'double dividends' from tax reforms and also the marginal costs of current taxes. Only a few of these studies consider environmental damages. The results of these indicate a net efficiency gain from introducing a carbon tax. Although none of the studies analyzes the impact on unemployment, a general conclusion is that there are efficiency gains associated with decreases in the payroll tax. Results show that marginal costs are relatively high for labour income and payroll taxes and low for VAT.

In order to achieve cost effectiveness, environmental charges, such as a CO_2 charge, should be uniform across all types of carbon emission sources, regions and sectors, and related to the carbon content. These cost effective criteria are not fulfilled in Norway or in any other country. There are in general several exemptions from tax liability. There are thus potential efficiency gains associated with a general carbon tax.

Two types of calculations were carried out: partial sector analyses and macroeconomic modelling. The partial studies calculated the potential increases in fiscal income from introductions or increases in environmental charges and reductions in subsidies with environmental damages. These are rather crude calculations. The potential incomes from different charges are presented in Table 2.2.

Table 2.2   Potential fiscal revenues from charges

Taxes	Millions of NOK
Rent taxes on:	
Power production	1 400
Fish	1 500
Forests	1 600
Environmental taxes on:	
Carbon	820
Sulphur	200
Waste	800-1 200
Transport	3 257-4 007
Total	8 777 - 10 727

Source: NOU 1996.

According to the table, the largest potential income source is transport, of which car charges account for about 2 000 million NOK.

In addition to the taxes in the table further potential tax bases were discussed: emission permits for ships and ship transports, metals and chemicals. The identification of desirable reductions in subsidies resulted in a calculation of current subsidies, but associated environmental impacts were not possible to determine. The direct subsidies amount to 20 300 million Nkr. The agricultural sector receives about 85-90 per cent of these subsidies. This sector has undoubtedly negative environmental impact and a reduction in subsidies would therefore probably increase environmental benefits. Other sectors receiving subsidies and with negative environmental impact are transport, tourism, fishery, forestry and defence.

Macro economic modelling indicates that a carbon charge of 50 NOK/ton without exemption generates in principle no employment effects and minor impact on GDP. An increase to 360 will, in the long run after about 10-15 years, increase the level of employment by 0.4 per cent but also decrease GDP by 0.3 per cent. In both cases the carbon charge was used to reduce the payroll tax. A simulation of a budget neutral increase in consumer energy prices turned out to have similar employment impacts, but also generated a small increase in GDP.

2.4 SUMMARY OF THE COMMISSION PROPOSALS

The Commission forecast of about a 30 per cent increase in the emission of CO_2 during a period of 15 years from 1995 in the absence of any environmental polices, constitutes an urgent request for counteracting policies. A tax reform implying an increase in environmental charges or reduced subsidies on environmentally harming activities, and recycling the revenues to cut taxes on labour is one such strategic policy. This is also in line with the Norwegian aim to instigate environmental policies in an international perspective. However, the Commission's work not only elucidated issues of principle, but also raised further, more concrete, questions. Therefore, the Commission summary is divided into principles for CO_2 charges, concrete charge suggestions, and suggestions that need further investigation.

The design of CO_2 charges was given much attention because it is regarded as one of the most important environmental policy tools in Norway. At an international level, it is also important to argue for cost effective programmes. Simulation results indicate that an inefficient program for international CO_2 reductions will have a more damaging impact on the Norwegian growth than cost effective emission reductions. However, the Commission members did not have the same view on the design of CO_2 charges. Most members argued that the basis for the Norwegian charges is the role as an international environmental promoter and commitments made by the signing of the UN climate convention. Only when a large group of countries cooperate, such as the OECD members, will the global CO_2 emission be of concern for Norwegian policies. They also suggest that the charge should be determined with respect to carbon content in all goods without exemption. A few members disagreed on this last point and held the opinion that the current exemptions should remain in place to avoid deterioration of competitiveness as compared with countries without similar charges.

2.4.1 Recommendations that can be implemented in the short run

The opinion of the Commission is that certain charges have been subjected to enough investigation and can be implemented in the short run. Such charges involve emissions of CO_2, SO_2, fuel for transports, and cars. The potential revenue from these charges should be used to decrease the payroll tax and labour market policies should be applied for reducing the level of unemployment. More precisely the suggestions on which most Commission members agreed are as follows:

- a CO_2 tax on the content of carbon amounting to 50 Nkr/kg for sectors which are exempt from the current charge system;
- a broadening of the base of SO_2 charges by imposing a charge of 5 Nkr/kg on new sources. A market system of tradable emission quotas where the initial permits are auctioned off could also be considered;
- harmonization of taxes on petroleum and diesel fuels, whereby the diesel charge is increased in order to correspond to the petroleum charge and introduced on buses' use of diesel;
- introduction of a charge on gas driven cars;
- harmonization of purchase taxes on automobiles whereby the charges on heavy cars are increased;
- reductions in current subsidies should be considered in the near future. Examples are transport subsidies to agriculture, construction of forest roads, mining at Svalbard, and freight subsidies with respect to petroleum products.

2.4.2 Suggestions that need further operationalizations:

- tax on studded tyres;
- differentiation of the annual charge on heavy vehicles;
- deposit refund system for waste;
- charge on packages for beverages;
- charge on final waste treatment of about 200-300 Nkr/ton;
- differentiated annual charge on leisure boats;
- introduction of charges on cadmium, nickel, trichloroethylene, and antibiotics for fish.

2.4.3   Suggestions that need further investigation

- road charges, which are of main interest for local environmental problems;
- charges on emission permits;
- further charges on aircraft noise;
- differentiated charges on ships and ship transports;
- a nature charge, which implies payments for environmentally harmful and changes of use.

In addition, the Commission also considers differentiated road pricing, less generous deductions of travel expenses for tax purposes, and a more efficient taxation of electricity. It is also suggested that an investigation on the potential of taxing rents in the fishery and forestry sectors are carried out. An evaluation of labour market measures for groups with particular difficulties in finding jobs are also suggested.

REFERENCE

NOU (Norges Offentlige Utredninger), 1996. *Grønne skatter - en politikk for bedre miljø og høj sysselsetting,* Statens Forvaltningestjeneste Statens trykning, Oslo, 1996:9

3. The Swedish Green Tax Commission
Runar Brännlund

3.1 INTRODUCTION

The Swedish Green Tax Commission was appointed by the government in March 1995, and the deadline for presenting its final report was January 1997. The Commission is a parliamentary Commission, which means that its members are representatives of the Swedish parliament. Apart from the members of parliament, the Commission consists of experts from various institutions and organizations such as trade unions, the Swedish Industry Federation, the Swedish Environmental Protection Agency, universities and so on. In brief, the Commission was asked whether Sweden should continue its 'greening' of the tax system. If so, what would the effects be on different parts of the economy as well as the effects on the environment? More specifically the terms of reference for the Commission can be summarized as follows (SOU 1997:11):

The Commission shall analyse the effects of the energy and environmentally related taxes currently in force. More specifically, according to the terms of reference given to the Commission, the Commission should study the effects on:

- the environment,
- the competitiveness,
- employment,
- efficiency in resource allocation,
- aggregate tax revenues.

One of the main tasks of the Commission's work is directed towards an evaluation of the prevailing economic instruments used in Swedish environmental policy. According to the terms of reference, special attention should be devoted to issues which are of particular interest for an analysis of revenue neutral tax reforms. The Commission shall analyse the conditions for and effects of different kinds of revenue neutral tax reforms.

The analysis shall consider both existing and new environmental taxes. In the analysis of the conditions for revenue neutral tax reforms it is important to investigate the 'stability' of the corresponding tax bases. When it comes to effects of the various tax reforms the Commission should put specific emphasis on:

- tax wedges,
- labour supply,
- employment,
- competitiveness,
- structural change,
- the environment.

These effects should be analysed both in short and long term perspectives. Specific attention should be given to transition effects. In other words, how the path of adjustment to a new 'equilibrium' will look.

The Commission introduced additional dimensions and issues to the analysis. These dimensions included effects on various aggregates of the economy, as well as a spatial dimension. Furthermore, the Commission also attempts to shed light on distributional and dynamic issues, as well as the taxation of natural resources. The point of departure for the Commission is that any tax changes would be revenue neutral, i.e., more tax revenues due to higher or new green taxes must be offset by a reduction of some other tax.

The Commission employed different vehicles in order to fulfil its task. These can be arranged into three different groups:

(i) Descriptive studies and surveys of the tax systems currently at work in Sweden and other OECD countries, as well as surveys in order to identify major environmental problems. Within this group a study was undertaken to investigate how people value environmental goods.

(ii) Partial, or sector, analysis of impacts of taxes. This includes studies on household and industry behaviour due to changes in the tax system.

(iii) General equilibrium analysis of various green tax reforms.

3.2 ENVIRONMENTAL PROBLEMS IN SWEDEN

According to the Commission, environmental problems can be divided in three main categories: global, regional and local problems. Examples of global problems are global warming and ozone depletion. The problem with global warming can mainly be attributed to the use of fossil fuels, whereas the ozone depletion problem is associated with CFC emissions. The problems are defined as 'global' since damages are independent of the location of the emission source. Currently, Sweden is emitting 60 million tons of carbon dioxide, which amounts to less than 4 per millage of global emission. In Table 3.1 it can be seen that there has been a considerable reduction since 1970. The Commission judges the global warming problem to be one of the most challenging threats for the future. The ozone depletion problem is of course a serious threat, but use of CFC's and HFC's have been prohibited in Sweden since 1996.

The main regional environmental problems are, according to the Commission, acidification of land and water, reduction of biodiversity, eutrophication, ground layer ozone and emissions of metals. Acidification derives from emissions of sulphur and nitrogen oxides. The problem of ground layer ozone originates to a large extent from emissions from traffic. Eutrophication has since the 1980s become a major problem for some specific land ecosystems along the Swedish coast. The causes of these problems can mainly be found in the emissions of nitrogen and phosphorous, which to a large extent originates from agriculture and sewage. Concerning emissions of metals the main part originates from abroad. Domestic emissions are mostly due to non-point sources such as household waste. According to the Commission, biodiversity is threatened by changes in land use.

Local environmental problems are to a large extent connected to problems in urban areas. Most of these problems are due to traffic, such as noise and air quality.

In Table 3.1 it can be seen that emissions of most substances have declined radically since 1970. This does not mean that there are any environmental problems since many of these problems are associated with these substances depend on how much is accumulated in the ecosystems and not in the flow. The development of biodiversity is not listed, mostly due to the fact that it does not exist in any great amount. It should also be noted that the development of non-point source emissions, such as nitrogen, are less positive than the development of many other emissions.

3.3 ENVIRONMENTAL AND ENERGY TAXES IN SWEDEN

Economic instruments in environmental policy have only recently been generally accepted as viable instruments in Sweden. In the 1970s, large subsidies were given to firms and local government to facilitate and speed up environmental protection measures. In particular, municipal waste water treatment plants were developed and extended during this period. This subsidisation scheme explains a major part of the substantial improvements in local environmental quality. Subsidies only play a minor role today. Subsidies

Table 3.1   Emissions of some substances, 1970-95

Substances	1970	1975	1980	1985	1990	1995
CO_2, Mton	120	139	82	65	59	58
SO_2, Kton	920	690	485	280	128	103
NO_x, Kton	300	320	320	320	406	383
VOC, Kton	600	560	b	450	500	500
Mercury (air, ton)	18	7	6	6	1.4	1
Mercury (water, ton)	16	1	3	1	0.2	b
Cadmium (air, ton)	38	12	12	5	2	1[a]
Cadmium (water, ton)	12	4	6	2	2	b
Led (air, ton)	3000	1300	1300	950	540	365[c]
Led (water, ton)	330	70	160	24	14	b
BOD[a], Kton	790	490	280	220	210	210
Suspended solids, Kton	340	180	140	85	b	b
Phosphorous (water, Kton)	16	13	8	5	3.5	3.5
Nitrogen, Kton	127	b	135	135	90	90

Source: 1997:11.

[a] BOD is biological oxygen demand, [b] missing value, [c] 1992 number.

exist for development of new technology, subsidies for liming of lakes, and a subsidy for the preservation of the cultural landscape.

A major emphasis came with the appointment of the Commission of Environmental Charges in 1988. It was part of a major tax reform. A total of SEK 19 000 million was transferred from income taxation to environmental and energy taxes. The Commission produced a large number of proposals in its interim reports (SOU 1989:21, SOU 1989:23) and in its final report (SOU 1990:59). The Commission was to analyse the scope for using economic measures in environmental policy on a large scale. Some of the proposals were accepted by parliament, and a number of environmental charges came into force on 1 January 1991. Table 3.2 lists the most important environmental taxes in current use.

The tax on CO_2 was introduced on 1 January 1991, at the level of 0.25 SEK/kg of CO_2 released. It is levied on oil, coal, natural gas, liquefied petroleum gas, petrol and aviation fuel in domestic traffic. There are exceptions on ethanol/methanol/biofules, peat, and waste. As from 1 January 1996, the tax has risen to 0.37 SEK/kg of emitted CO_2, but after the energy tax reform in 1993, the manufacturing industry pays only 25 per cent of the amount for competitive reasons. Note that the tax varies over fuels and that it is an input tax. Invariably, environmental taxes are constructed as taxes on inputs, because of the difficulty of constructing a pure emission tax. Roughly, the CO_2 tax corresponds to about USD 200/tons of carbon. According to the Commission of Environmental Charges (SOU 1990:59), USD 200 is the marginal cost for achieving stabilisation of CO_2 emissions at the 1988 level (a goal that, incidentally, has been abolished).

The sulphur tax of January 1991 focuses on sulphur content in oil, coal, and peat (exceptions are crude and waste oil). The sulphur tax was introduced with the aim of reducing sulphur emissions by 80 per cent, using 1980 as a baseline. This aim is likely to have been met. The sulphur charge is SEK 30/kg S, which is roughly 4 USD.

The charge on nitrogen oxide emissions (NO_x) is focused on reducing emissions by 30 per cent, using 1985 as the base year. It is levied on domestic air traffic (12 SEK/kg NO_x, introduced in 1989) and large combustion plants (40 SEK/kg NO_x introduced in 1992). The tax on domestic air traffic has, however, been abandoned from 1 January 1997. The NO_x charge on combustion plants has two interesting features. First, it is the only emission charge levied in Sweden; NO_x emissions are monitored at the large plants and

Table 3.2   Main environmental taxes in Sweden 1996

Type of tax	Tax rate
Electricity tax	industry: 0 others: 0.09 SEK/kWh
Energy tax on fossil fuels	petrol: 3.30 SEK/litre oil for heating: 0.59 SEK/litre other: 0.37 SEK/kg (petrol: 0.87 SEK/litre)
Sulphur tax	30 SEK/kg
Producer tax on electricity	hydro power: 0.04 SEK/kWh nuclear power: 0,012 SEK/kWh
Tax on nitrogen in fertilizers	1.80 sek/kg N
Tax on pesticides	20 SEK/kg active substance
Tax on gravel	5 SEK/ton
Tax on domestic air traffic (No tax from 1 January 1997)	CO_2 1SEK/litre Hydrocarbons 12 SEK/kg Nitrogen oxides 12 SEK/NO_x
Charge on nitrogen oxides	40 SEK/kg No_x (large scale combustion)
Battery charge	led: 40 SEK/battery alk: 23 SEK/kg nicd: 25 SEK/kg
'Junk' car charge	1 300 SEK/car

taxed accordingly. Second, because monitoring all combustion plants is too expensive, the tax revenues have to be returned to the liable plants as a group to avoid unfair competition between small and large plants. The income from the charge is refunded to the large plants according to their energy efficiency. In this way, the scheme provides the individual plant with incentives to invest in cleaner technology.

Tax differentiation on diesel fuels was introduced in January 1991 with the purpose of stimulating the use (and production) of environmentally superior grades of diesel oil. There are three environmental classes of diesel, where the parameters for classification are maximum sulphur content, maximum aromatic hydrocarbon content, maximum polycyclic aromatic hydrocarbons, and certain other parameters. Technically, it is the energy tax that differs among the classes. Class 1 has an energy tax of 90 SEK/m^3, class 2 has 2 290 SEK/m^3, and class 3 has 540 SEK/m^3. From an environmental point of view this was a success. Already in 1992 50 per cent of total diesel sales belonged to class 1 or 2. In 1993 the figure was 80 per cent.

Table 3.3 lists revenues from taxes that have a clear environmental profile, and some other excise taxes which are environmentally related. It should be clear from Table 3.3 that, in terms of revenues, taxes on energy are far the most important.

3.4 ANALYTICAL TOOLS AND SUMMARY OF THE RESULTS

One of the main objectives for the Swedish Green Tax Commission has been to assess whether environmentally related taxes have been efficient or not, in terms of reducing the negative load on the environment. To achieve this the Commission uses various tools, such as partial equilibrium models for the household and industry sector as well as a numerical general equilibrium model for the entire Swedish economy. The simple idea adopted by the Commission is that tax increases on various goods lead to higher consumer prices. Thus, by studying changes in consumer/producer behaviour with respect to price changes, the effects of taxes can be deduced. The Commission concludes that environmental taxes, such as carbon dioxide tax and sulphur tax, have the intended effect in the sense that higher taxes reduce emissions. However, the effects turn out to be quite small, at least in the short run. As a consequence of this it turns out that the carbon dioxide tax is a fairly stable tax base.

A second objective of the Swedish Green Tax Commission is to evaluate and analyse various green tax reforms. Since a main issue in the Commission's work is to establish the likelihood for a double dividend of

*Table 3.3   Revenues from environmental and environmentally related
             taxes, million SEK*

Taxes and charges	1996
Energy taxes on fossil fuels	23 770
Carbon dioxide tax on fossil fuels	12 900
Sulphur tax	190
Electricity tax (consumption tax)	6 270
Producer tax on hydro electric power	1 358
Producer tax on nuclear power	920
Tax on domestic air traffic	192
Total energy related taxes	*46 050*
Sales vehicle tax	1 370
Vehicle tax	4 946
Total vehicle tax	*6 316*
Tax on fertilizers and pesticides	317
Tax on gravel	106
Nitrogen oxides	0
Battery charge	29
'Junk' car charge	0
Total environmentally related taxes and charges	*452*
Total energy and environmental taxes	*52 818*
Share of GDP	3.2%
Share of total tax revenues	6%

further 'greening' of the tax system various scenarios are analysed. The
analysis is conducted both within a partial and general equilibrium framework
(see Harrison and Kriström in this volume). The main conclusion from this
analysis is that it is not very likely that there exist any double dividend in
addition to the environmental effects. This conclusion rests to a large extent
on two basic facts. First of all, environmental and energy tax rates are
relatively high in Sweden. Second, revenues from environmental energy taxes
are relatively small compared to total revenues. Combined, these two facts
indicates the difficulty of obtaining any substantial reduction of 'other' taxes
by raising environmental and energy taxes. A second conclusion from the
analysis is that a further 'greening' of the tax system, in terms of a revenue
neutral tax shift tend to be regressive, i.e. low income households are

relatively worse off than high income households. Furthermore, the Commission concludes that the structural change will be a consequence of a tax shift which will probably have a negative impact on regional income distribution, which has to be accounted for.

3.5 PROPOSALS AND RECOMMENDATIONS FROM THE COMMISSION

The main conclusion from the Commission is that Sweden has secured environmental improvements in a number of areas. This has been accomplished partly by an increase in the use of economic instruments within the general reshaping of the Swedish tax system. The general recommendation from the Commission is that Sweden should continue this reshaping process. The Commission does not propose any specific tax reforms. Instead, the Commission proposes some overarching principles which should guide future policy in this area. These principles are briefly presented below:

Sweden should pursue its active role in the international efforts to combat global and regional environmental problems. But a condition to pursue this strategy is that other countries do the same. Another condition is that the chosen policy can show positive results on the national level. The Commission states that Sweden cannot be viewed as a 'good example' to the rest of the world if the measures taken in Sweden imply that production is moved to other countries with less stringent environmental policies. More specifically the Commission suggests more joint action between countries, and promotion to research and development in order to increase the use of renewable energy sources. To achieve this, Sweden should actively use its European Union membership, according to the Commission. Given a common European Union climate policy and a long-term energy policy, Sweden should promote the establishment, during 1997, of a protocol that would detail a timetable for emission reductions and emission targets. The Commission proposes that a joint and expanded Nordic cooperation in the environmental area should be promoted. Informal cooperation is of particular value in this endeavour. The recently accepted Nordic environmental strategy underlines the need for close cooperation in the preparations of the 1997 UN special session, as well as in the development of global conventions. The Commission also emphasises the importance of cooperation with Eastern Europe and countries around the Baltic Sea.

Furthermore, the Commission states that a Swedish green tax reform has to take into consideration how investments, economic growth and equity are affected. In addition, regional effects within Sweden have to be considered whenever environmental taxes are introduced or are subject to change.

According to the Commission, any green tax reform may call for measures in order to prevent undesirable effects. One such measure is to target tax cuts to compensate for possible negative distributional impacts.

The Commission also recommends that revenues obtained through environmental or other taxes should in general not be designated. Each dollar of tax-revenue should be used where its utility is highest. A conclusion from the Commission is that additional revenues from energy and environmental taxes will not leave room for any substantial general decrease of labour taxes. By this reason, revenues from a green tax reform should be used selectively. Tax cuts which will have the largest effects on unemployment should have first priority.

To conclude, the Commission recommends that Sweden should pursue its active role in order to achieve global, regional, and local environmental improvements. However, it is also recognized by the Commission that Sweden is a small open economy which means that this cannot be done alone without jeopardising the competitiveness of the Swedish economy. As is pointed out by the Commission, Sweden has already taken significant steps in reshaping the tax systems. The tax reform of 1991 is an example of this.

REFERENCE

SOU (Statens Offentliga Utredningar), (1997), '*Skatter, miljö och sysselsättning*', Slutbetänkande från Skatteväxlingskommittén, Stockholm, 1997:11.

4.   Double Dividend: Just Desserts or Pie in the Sky?

David Starrett

The possibility of a 'double dividend' has generated considerable confusion in the recent discussion concerning green taxes. I will try to explain the origins of this confusion and the current state of thinking on the subject as reflected in the chapters presented in this volume. Then, I will assess the potential for finding inexpensive or even costless ways of imposing green taxes.

The idea behind double dividend claims is as follows: In almost all western economies, the tax systems in place are distortionary in that they restrict activity in tax markets below what would be first best optimal. Therefore, the imposition of externality correcting taxes (which are justified anyway on first best grounds) can be used to reduce taxes in such markets and thereby generate an economic dividend through reduced distortion costs, quite apart from their beneficial effects on the environment.

I will discuss these issues using the methodology of second best welfare measures in the mixed economy. The context is one in which a relatively large sector of the economy is governed by market allocation, but various aspects of this allocation are second best relative to the most efficient and equitable allocation possible. Contributing second best factors include inequitable distribution, indirect taxation, monopoly power, quantity constraints and the like. We focus first on the case where the only distortions are due to indirect taxation and comment later on corrections that must be made when other distortions are present.

Suppose that there is a consumption good (x) which generates negative externalities (pollution) and we consider a policy that raises the tax rate (t_x) on that commodity and lowers some other tax in a revenue neutral way. Assuming that the resulting changes are small, it can be shown that the resulting change in welfare (dW) normalized in numeraire units can be expressed as[1]

---

1   This methodology is summarized and justified in Starrett (1988).

$$dW = -\Omega dx + \sum_{goods}(tax\ rates)\cdot(d\ tax\ base) \qquad (4.1)$$

where Ω stands for the marginal social damages caused by pollution in the status quo ante (before the policy change), dx is the change in the level of good x induced by the policy change and $d\ tax\ base$ is the analogous change for other taxed goods.

Consider a model in which there are only three goods: the 'dirty' good (x), a clean consumption good (c), and leisure good (n); the tax system consists of taxes on consumption as in the context of Diamond and Mirrlees (1971). If all three goods could be taxed, it is well known that a uniform tax rate would be lump sum in nature and therefore first best. However, it is difficult to see how leisure can be effectively taxed, which is the main reason most economists think that lump sum taxation is infeasible. Therefore, we treat leisure as an untaxed good; then, normalizing so that producer good prices are unity,[2] a typical consumer budget constraint takes the form

$$(1+t_c)c+(1+t_x)x+n = N \qquad (4.2)$$

where N stands for labour endowment, I believe that this is the model in mind when the intuitive argument for a double divided was first put forth. The associated intuition is as follows. If good c is taxed and good x is not, the environmental tax when instituted will cause a smaller distortion in its own market than the distortion alleviated by reducing the tax on c. Let us see if we can quantify this intuition.

We start with a status quo in which the tax rates are at some given ex ante levels and consider a change in which the tax on x is raised slightly and that on c is lowered in a revenue neutral way. Assuming this induces 'first order' changes in market variables, the formula above applies and we measure the change in welfare as:

$$dW = -\Omega dx + t_x dx + t_c dc = (t_x - \Omega)dx + t_c dc \qquad (4.3)$$

Using these expressions, we can give precise meaning to the various concepts of double dividend. If $t_c dc > 0$, so that $dW > (t_x-\Omega)dx$, we say that there is a *positive double dividend*. When this is true, taxing commodity x confers some extra benefits by reducing distortions, in that benefits from increasing the tax exceed what they would be in a first best world (where it is desirable to raise the tax until it is exactly equal to the marginal social cost of pollution). In this situation, it is desirable to restrict pollution somewhat

---

2   We are implicitly assuming here that producer goods prices are fixed and do not change when taxes are adjusted.

below the level that would be justified in a first-best world by setting the tax rate somewhat above what it would be in that world.

If $t_x dx + t_c dc \geq 0$, so that $dW \geq -\Omega dx$, we say that there is a *strong double dividend*. In this case the tax swap is so effective at reducing distortions that the policy imposes no tax costs at all and the tax increase on commodity x is desirable as long as it confers environmental benefit no matter how small. Thus, the optimal policy here will be to raise the tax on x at least far enough to reduce the marginal environmental benefit to zero.

Although the presence of these dividends can never be established without some assumption about relative elasticities, we will argue that there is a strong presumption for a positive double dividend in this case. Think about the likely effects of a tax swap whereby t_x is raised and t_c is lowered. Under normal circumstances with own price effects dominating cross price effects, we expect $dx<0$ and $dc>0$. In fact, if the first of these inequalities did not hold, the policy would have the distinctly perverse and undesirable effect of rasing rather than lowering the level of pollution. Assuming, as seems reasonable, that the clean consumption good is a relatively large aggregate while the dirty good is relatively small in the economy, the compensating change in t_c is relatively small and we would find $dx>0$ only if the own price effect on dirty good demand is positive. We assume away this unlikely possibility.

The second of the inequalities above ($dc>0$) implies a positive double dividend. To justify it carefully, we decompose the relevant tax term into two parts as follows:

$$t_c dc = t_c \frac{\partial c}{\partial t_x} + t_c \frac{\partial c}{\partial t_c} \frac{\partial t_c}{\partial t_x} \tag{4.4}$$

where the first term measures the direct effect on demand for c from the increase in tax on x, and is called the *tax interaction effect* in the work of Bovenberg and Goulder, whereas the second term measures the indirect effect through the revenue neutral tax swap which lowers the tax on c; this term is called the *revenue recycling effect* by Bovenberg and Goulder[3]. Under normal conditions on preferences and technology, both of these terms will be positive in the present circumstances, If goods x and c are normal substitutes, we expect an increase in tax on x to increase the demand for c, so the tax interaction effect will be positive. Similarly, the tax swap derivative is negative and the own tax effect on c should be negative, so the revenue recycling effect is positive as well.

Thus, under normal assumptions we would see a positive double dividend

---

3   These terms are used in papers presented at this workshop but were actually introduced earlier. See Goulder (1994) for a survey of previous work.

in this situation. It is less likely, though possible that we would see a strong double dividend. For this to occur we must have $t_c dc > t_x(-dx)$, that is, the positive effects of the tax swap on the clean consumption tax base would have to more than compensate for the presumed negative effects on the dirty good tax base; demand for c would have to be relatively more elastic than that for x so that the optimal tax on c is lower than on x. Bovenberg and Goulder have given numerical examples for similar models where this does in fact happen, but the case is not nearly as compelling as that for a positive double dividend.

Given the arguments above, why have we seen rather pessimistic analyses as to the likelihood of double dividends? The reason is that tax systems imposed in most countries do not look much like the one just analysed, and the presence of double dividends is quite sensitive to the status quo ante tax system. To see this, consider the model in which the main tax is on labour income (as it is in most extant tax systems) at rate T_n. Then representative budget constraint takes the form:

$$c + (1 + T_x) x = (1 - T_n)(N - n) \qquad (4.5)$$

where T_x is the proposed green tax to be added. Here we see that a tax on labour can usefully be interpreted as inducing a subsidy to leisure relative to its treatment in the previous tax systems studied. Applying our general formula for welfare change to this situation,[4] we find

$$dW = -\Omega dx + T_x dx - T_n dn = (T_x - \Omega)dx - T_n dn \qquad (4.6)$$

A positive change dn means a negative change in labour income tax base; hence the minus sign in this expression. Expanding the term now relevant for a positive double dividend, we find:

$$- T_n dn = - T_n \frac{\partial n}{\partial T_x} - T_n \frac{\partial n}{\partial T_n} \frac{\partial T_n}{\partial T_x} \qquad (4.7)$$

The revenue recycling effect should still be positive since the tax swap derivative is always negative while an increase in the labour tax should increase the demand for leisure. Indeed, this result is quite general and reflects the fact that we are always better off using the green tax revenue to reduce some other distorting tax rather then (for example) returning it in a lump sum manner.[5] However, now the tax interaction effect is negative as

---

4   Note that $dN = 0$ since labour endowment is fixed exogenously.
5   This proposition is a restatement of the fact that indirect taxation is costly relative to lump sum taxation and as such is well established in the literature. A positive revenue recycling effect is referred to as a *weak double dividend* in the earlier work of Bovenberg and Goulder.

long as leisure and the dirty good are substitutes. Therefore, the net effect depends on which of these terms is larger in absolute value.

It turns out that for a 'neutral' specification of parameters, the tax interaction term dominates so that the double dividend is actually negative. The best way to get some intuition for this result is to convert the labour tax system into one directly comparable to our original consumption tax framework, namely one in which leisure is untaxed rather than subsidized. Dividing through by factor $1-T_n$ generates the equivalent budget constraint

$$\frac{1}{1-T_n}c + \frac{1+T_x}{1-T_n}x + n = N \tag{4.8}$$

It follows that the labour tax is equivalent to a consumption tax in which the tax rate on clean and dirty consumption are respectively;

$$t_c = \frac{1}{1-T_n} - 1 = \frac{T_n}{1-T_n}$$

$$\tag{4.9}$$

$$t_x = \frac{1+T_x}{1-T_n} - 1 = \frac{T_x + T_n}{1-T_n}$$

We see that the dirty good is already 'effectively' taxed in the status quo ante relative to the untaxed good, leisure. Adding an explicit green tax raises this effective rate above that on the clean good. Assuming that the clean and dirty goods are average substitutes for leisure, a single labour tax is second best optimal and adding an explicit green tax must worsen the second best cost of taxation -hence the negative double dividend.

Recent calculations of the double dividend potential (as represented in the workshop papers by Bovenberg and Goulder) have started with a tax system dominated by the labour tax, which explains why they have generally been pessimistic about the potential for a positive double dividend. Of course, it is still possible with the right elasticity assumptions to get a positive double dividend. For example, if the dirty good does not substitute for leisure (so that all substitution is between the clean good and leisure) then the tax interaction effect is zero and there is indeed a positive double dividend. This possibility has also been quantified by Bovenberg and Goulder. We could also get a positive double dividend if the dirty good happens to be *subsidized* in the status quo ante (that is, $T_x < 0$); then, even if both goods are average substitutes for leisure, raising the tax (reducing the subsidy) on the dirty good generates a second best improvement. It might be argued that this last situation applies in the US economy for commodities like grazing and mining rights, which many economists argue are effectively subsidized.

The above analysis does suggest, however, one sense in which there is always a positive double dividend. If we normalize as above to convert an extant tax system into an equivalent one in which all taxes are assessed on consumption (with leisure untaxed), then the optimal *consumption* tax rate on the dirty good generally will exceed the marginal environmental damages. In this sense, the intuition we suggested at the outset is correct. However, when taxes are assessed on the income side of the ledger (as with a labour income tax) the equivalent consumption tax is an artificial construction and the dividend associated with the *actual* tax rate is very likely to be negative as we have seen.

Several generalizations can be made here. First, whenever the status quo ante tax system is second best optimal, addition of a green tax must worsen the distortion costs of taxation and lead to a negative double dividend. Only if the dirty good is effectively taxed too low relative to some other clean good that is taxed too high can a tax swap be made that leads to positive double dividends. This latter condition holds in the labour tax world if the clean good happens to substitute highly with leisure whereas the dirty good does not. Aside from such conditions on relative elasticities which seem unlikely and are in any event difficult to establish empirically, any search for positive double dividend must identify some good which is taxed at a considerably higher effective rate than the dirty one in the status quo ante tax system.

Two issues arise in conducting the associated research: First, can such an overtaxed commodity be found? And second, if so would it be politically feasible to make a tax swap using that commodity? The second question is important since if the tax system is out of alignment there would be grounds for making a correction quite apart from the desirability of green taxes. And if the correction has not been made, there may be reasons based on other objectives or political constraints. Only if the tax planners were ignorant of the excess distortion can a 'something for nothing' tax swap be arranged.

As an example, suppose we find that due to the double taxation of savings in our income tax, future consumption is overtaxed in the sense above. Then the associated tax swap would involve reducing the capital gains tax (or other taxes on saving income) and substituting a carbon tax. This swap would undoubtedly be resisted on equity grounds: it would reduce the burden on the rich at the expense of an increase on the poor. In this case, the ex ante excess distortion has been justified by another objective (equity) which has been left out of our calculations. And just as before, if the status quo ante is second best optimal taking both efficiency and equity considerations into account, we cannot expect to generate a free ride in connection with the introduction of green taxes.

There are other second best distortions (aside from indirect taxation and equity) that might affect relative desirability of green taxes. The most likely candidate is effective quantity constraints in the labour market (that is, involuntary unemployment). To the extent that the labour market does not make clear, the value of an extra employment unit in our welfare measure will be higher than the tax rate since the marginal value of leisure is lower than the after tax wage.[6] This factor could influence the double dividend calculus in either direction. If the employment constraints are rigid and little influenced by the addition of green taxes then there will be minimal 'lost employment' costs and the double dividend is more likely to be positive. However, each unit of employment lost has a higher welfare cost than previously, so the negative dividend could be even larger than before if employment levels are affected.

In conclusion, it seems quite doubtful that green taxes can be justified solely on the basis of improvements they facilitate in the welfare cost of taxation. Rather, they must be justified on their merits as vehicles for reducing environmental damage. If anything, it seems likely that green taxes should actually be held to somewhat higher standard than they would be in a first best world, since they worsen (at the margin) the second best distortions from indirect taxation under reasonable assumptions about the underlying tax systems. However, regardless of which way the second best considerations point, they are almost certain to be of second order importance compared to getting the pollution control level in the right perspective.

REFERENCES

Diamond, P. and Mirrles, J. (1971), 'Optimal taxation and public production', *American Economic Review*, Vol. **61**, pp. 8-27, 261-78.

Goulder, L. (1995), 'Environmental taxation and the 'Double dividend': A reader's guide', *International Tax and Public Finance*, Vol. **2**, pp. 157-83.

Starrett, D. (1988), *Foundations of Public Economics*, Cambridge University Press.

---

6 Precise formulas that account for such quantity constraints are derived in Starrett (op. cit) Ch. 9.

5 Green Tax Reform: Theoretical Issues, Empirical Results, and Future Challenges

Lawrence H. Goulder

In this chapter I shall discuss what we have learned from numerical models - and especially from CGE models - about the economic impacts of green tax reforms. I shall also sketch out some areas for fruitful future research on such reforms. But to put things in perspective, I would like first to summarize some main theoretical results. This will help motivate the numerical experiments and provide a rationale for the suggestions about future studies.

The chapter is organized as follows: Section 5.1 articulates some recent and significant theoretical results relating to green tax reforms. Section 5.2 presents issues in numerical modelling of such reforms, while Section 5.3 outlines results from a sampling of numerical models. The final section indicates policy implications that emerge from the recent theoretical and empirical findings, and outlines promising areas for future research.

5.1 WHAT WE KNOW FROM THEORY

Let us focus on *revenue-neutral* green tax reforms, that is, reforms in which environmentally-motivated taxes (such as carbon taxes, Btu taxes on fossil fuels, or petroleum taxes) replace, in a revenue-neutral fashion, ordinary income or factor taxes. We can distinguish at least three potential 'dividends' from such a revenue-neutral swap:

1. improved environmental quality;
2. reduction in the gross costs of the tax system (where 'gross costs' denotes the costs before accounting for environmental-quality-related benefits);
3. increased employment of labour.

The first of these dividends is not controversial.[1] It is the second and third that provoke disagreement. In most of the rest of this discussion of theoretical background, I shall focus on the second potential dividend above and consider the key determinants it obtains.

Recent theoretical work[2] shows that the presence or absence of the second dividend depends on the strength and direction of three key effects:

(a)   the revenue recycling effect;
(b)   the tax interaction effect, and;
(c)   the tax shifting effect.

The revenue recycling effect is the cost reduction obtained by using the revenues from a green tax reform to cut an ordinary, distortionary tax - relative to the cost that would occur if the revenue were returned to the economy lump sum. The existence of this effect is not controversial. It can be shown that it follows from the definition of 'distortionary' tax.[3] A 'weak version' of the double-dividend hypothesis is simply the assertion that the revenue recycling effect exists, and thus the weak version is easy to confirm.

The tax interaction effect is less obvious. It is the cost increase from a green tax reform imposed in a second-best setting (with pre-existing factor taxes) *relative* to the cost that would occur if the green tax were imposed in a first-best setting with no pre-existing (factor) taxes. In general, the tax interaction effect works to raise costs; thus it works in the opposite direction from that of the revenue recycling effect.

5.1.1   Relative Size of the Tax Interaction and Revenue Recycling Effects

If we ignore (for the moment) the tax shifting effect, then the presence or absence of the second dividend above depends on whether the tax interaction effect is larger or smaller in absolute magnitude than the revenue recycling effect. Bovenberg and de Mooij (1994) have shown that, in a simple model with one primary factor (labour), the tax interaction effect is larger in magnitude - indicating that the double (or second) dividend fails to materialize.[4] The larger magnitude of the tax interaction effect reflects two phenomena:

---

1   Although nearly all studies assume or find that revenue-neutral green tax reforms will lead to a reduction in pollution. However, Schob (1994) identifies some (unusual) circumstances under which even this first dividend would not obtain.

2   See, for example, Bovenberg and de Mooij (1994), Bovenberg and van der Ploeg (1994), Parry (1995), and Bovenberg and Goulder (1996, 1997).

3   See Goulder (1995a).

4   See also Parry (1995). Parry was the first to decompose the impacts of revenue-neutral reforms into the tax-interaction and revenue-recycling effects, which he termed the

(1) the environmentally motivated tax is an implicit factor tax that generates the same factor-market distortion per dollar of revenue raised, as the explicit factor tax it replaces;

(2) the environmentally motivated tax, in addition to distorting factor markets, 'distorts' intermediate input choice or consumer good choice.

If only (1) above held, then the tax interaction effect would exactly match the revenue recycling effect. But the further 'distortion' indicated by (2) means that the tax interaction effect is larger in magnitude than the revenue recycling effect. The word 'distortion' is quoted to indicate that the misallocation is judged as abstracting from environmental benefits. Once environmental benefits are taken into account, the change in allocation implied by the environmental tax in the markets intermediate goods or consumer goods may be entirely justified in terms of overall efficiency.

The dominance of the tax interaction effect over the revenue recycling effect is a fairly robust result. Still, some underlying assumptions deserve attention. To obtain this result, analytical models usually assume that utility functions are homothetic and that goods are separable from leisure in utility. This prescribes any unevenness in the relative taxation of consumer goods. If these assumptions are dropped, an environmental tax in some instances could improve consumer good allocation (abstracting from environmental concerns) by changing the relative costs of consumer goods. Under these conditions, the tax interaction effect could be smaller than the revenue recycling effect, and if it were, the double (second) dividend would be obtained after all. For this to occur, the non-separability and non-homothetic nature of utility functions need to work in a way that justifies, on non-environmental grounds, relatively high taxes on polluting goods or services. Thus, in this case, the green tax reform is accomplishing an objective which is partly justified even in the absence of environmental considerations.[5] These considerations suggest the usefulness of further empirical studies to ascertain more closely the nature of consumer preferences. Are homotheticity and separability reasonable specifications for consumer utility functions?

5.1.2   The Tax-Shifting Effect

The tax-shifting effect is the influence on gross cost associated with the reform's impact on the relative taxation of labour and capital. This effect is analyzed in Bovenberg and Goulder (1997) and de Mooij and Bovenberg (1997). For this effect to take place, there must be some pre-existing discrepancy in the marginal (gross) excess burden of taxation of labour and capital: one factor is overtaxed, while the other is undertaxed. The tax shifting

interdependency and revenue effects.

5   A more detailed discussion of this issue is provided in Bovenberg and Goulder (1998).

effect can either work toward the second dividend, or work against it. To favour the second dividend, the combination of environmental tax and reduction in ordinary (income) tax must shift the burden of taxation from the overtaxed factor to the undertaxed one.

The tax shifting effect also bears on the third (employment) dividend above. In the simplest analytical models with only one primary factor (usually), there was no possibility of tax shifting. This meant that dividends 2 and 3 were fundamentally joined: either both materialized or neither one did. But when one allows for more than one primary factor, the connection between dividends 2 and 3 becomes looser. The employment dividend (3) is now somewhat easier to obtain than the cost dividend (2). In some cases, the tax shifting effect will not be strong enough to yield the cost dividend, but it will be sufficiently powerful to generate the employment dividend. This happens when revenue-neutral green tax reform shifts the tax burden from labour to capital, raising employment even though the overall costs of the tax system (measured in terms of the lost value of consumption and leisure) do not fall. In this circumstance, workers gain while owners of capital lose. To obtain the second dividend, in contrast, it is not sufficient that the tax burden be shifted. In addition, there must be a beneficial efficiency effect associated with such tax shifting large enough to overcome the negative net efficiency impact of the combination of tax interaction and revenue recycling effects.

These considerations point to a general principle that underlies the absence of the second dividend. In order for this dividend to materialize, there must be a pre-existing inefficiency *along non-environmental dimensions*. The presence of the tax shifting effect reflects one such inefficiency - an inefficiency in the relative taxation of labour and capital. We alluded briefly above to another potential inefficiency that would give scope for the second dividend: namely, a lack of separability in utility functions that favoured (on non-environmental grounds) the relatively high taxation of consumer goods or services associated with pollution. Other pre-existing inefficiencies - such as those associated with pre-existing subsidies to polluting activities, with the failure to exploit monopsony power (or terms-of-trade gains) on international markets, or with rigidities in labour markets - can offer scope for the second dividend. We shall not explore all of these cases here, but rather emphasize the general idea that the second dividend requires the presence of a non-environment-related inefficiency that is reduced through the environmental tax reform.[6] The question arises as to why one needs *green* tax reform to deal with these inefficiencies. This question raises important political issues that are beyond the scope of this chapter.

---

6 For a detailed discussion, see Goulder (1995a) and Bovenberg and Goulder (1998).

5.1.3 Empirical Issues Raised by the Theory

In my view, the theory has been extremely successful in clarifying the economic conditions necessary for dividends 2 or 3. In many ways, the onus is on the empirical modeller: empirical modellers need to ascertain the magnitudes of the various, often contrasting, effects. Some key questions generated by the theory are:

1. How large are pre-existing factor taxes, and how large is the tax interaction effect that stems from such taxes?
2. How large is the revenue recycling effect? That is, how much difference does it make to the gross costs if taxes are returned lump sum rather than cuts in distortionary taxes?
3. What is the direction and magnitude of the tax shifting effect? In which direction, and by how much, do green taxes shift the burden of taxation from one factor to another? What are the discrepancies in the marginal excess burdens of labour and capital (the discrepancies that influence the magnitude of the tax-shifting effect)? Does tax shifting work in favour of the second dividend or does it undermine it?
4. Does the second dividend materialize for important types of green tax reform?

These questions can only be answered empirically. In general they require the application of models that are too complex to be solved analytically; hence they motivate numerical modelling.

5.2 NUMERICAL MODELLING ISSUES

To answer the various questions posed by theory, the following features of numerical models seem especially important:

1. An integrated treatment of environmental taxes and (existing) distortionary taxes.

Since environmental taxes are implicit factor taxes, when environmental taxes are introduced in a setting where explicit factor taxes are already present, the environmental taxes function like increases in existing factor taxes. This implies that the gross costs of a new environmental tax depend on the magnitudes of the marginal rates of existing factor taxes. Hence the costs of environmental taxes very much depend on the configuration of ordinary taxes that exist prior to the imposition of the new environmental tax. To assess these costs, one needs a model that incorporates both types of taxes. CGE models are well suited to meet this need.

2. A close attention to behavioural responses to taxes, especially in energy industries.

Since welfare costs (deadweight losses) are determined by the elasticities of supply and demand, one needs to model carefully the responses to tax induced changes in relative prices. Many environmental taxes focus on energy fuels or products; hence a careful treatment of energy demands and supplies is most important.

3. Attention to the environmental benefits of green tax reform.

If one's mission is solely to determine the presence or absence of the second and third dividends, one need not consider the environmental impacts. But a more thorough assessment of green tax reform would involve a comparison of environmental benefits with the non-environmental costs. To ascertain the environmental benefits, one needs a model that captures the links from (1) producer and consumer activities to (2) emissions of major pollutants to (3) concentrations of major pollutants to (4) health and welfare impacts.

Some CGE models have emerged that capture some of these features. These include the OECD GREEN model, the Jorgenson-Wilcoxen model, and the Goulder model.[7] The Jorgenson-Wilcoxen and Goulder models are US models (with foreign trade), while the GREEN model is a global model with regional differentiation. How do these models fare along the above dimensions?

Integrated tax treatment. All three models include an integrated treatment of environmental and pre-existing distortionary taxes. The Jorgenson-Wilcoxen and Goulder models offer somewhat more detail on taxes than does GREEN. The treatment of taxes may be most challenging when it comes to dealing with capital taxation and the associated dynamic incentives. The Jorgenson-Wilcoxen model has recently been expanded to include a sophisticated, cost-of-capital approach to capital taxes. The Goulder model, in contrast, adopts the asset price framework of Summers. The asset price approach can be viewed as an extension of the cost-of-capital approach that takes account of adjustment costs associated with the installation of new capital. As mentioned later, the presence or absence of adjustment costs can have a significant bearing on the results from policy simulations because it influences the importance of the tax shifting effect.

Energy demand and supply. The models do fairly well in their treatments of energy demand. Two decades ago, Hudson and Jorgenson (1974) incorporated a flexible treatment of energy substitutions in a CGE model - allowing for substitutions between specific forms of energy and between

---

7 These models are described in detail in Burniaux *et al.* (1991), Jorgenson and Wilcoxen (1990, 1996), and Goulder (1995b).

energy as a whole and other inputs. This flexible treatment of energy demand is now routinely captured in CGE models. Virtually all of the CGE models addressing green tax reforms incorporate such features.

The treatment of energy supply is generally less satisfactory. Most CGE models ignore the non renewable or exhaustible nature of fossil fuel resources: traditionally, only optimization models have considered exhaustibility. In CGE models, energy industries are usually regarded as constant-returns-to-scale industries capable of producing output in unlimited quantities.

Capturing exhaustibility and the dynamics of non renewable resource supplies is important for two reasons. First, recognizing these dynamic affect the time profile of the energy tax base and of tax revenues. This in turn affects the extent to which environmentally motivated taxes or energy taxes can finance cuts in other taxes. Second, capturing these dynamics affects the elasticity of energy supply and the rents earned by owners of energy resources. To the extent that environmental taxes shift the tax burden from relatively elastically supplied factors (capital and labour) to inelastically supplied factors (energy resources), the gross costs of these taxes are reduced. Existing models, by ignoring energy resources (that is, stocks of energy reserves), may bias upward the assessment of the costs of green tax reforms, since they ignore the presence of a relatively inelastic primary factor.

The Goulder model is distinct in incorporating a forward-looking, intertemporally optimizing treatment of the oil and gas supply that accounts for the exhaustible nature of these fuels. It also incorporates a backstop substitute for oil and gas whose rate of market penetration is based on intertemporally optimizing. Further work to capture such resource dynamics in CGE models could have significant payoffs for the analysis of green tax reforms.

Environmental benefits. The existing stock of CGE models tends to concentrate on the cost side, disregarding the environment-related benefits. As everyone knows, fathoming the benefits is hard. It requires the establishing of links from industry or consumer activities to pollution generation to health and welfare impacts.

GREEN has begun to develop such links for greenhouse gases. Fossil fuel use is associated with emissions of various greenhouse gases. These then imply certain changes in concentrations and 'climate damage'. Many of the benefits from green tax reforms concern reductions in local pollutants. The Goulder model adopts an emissions factor approach to consider the implications of tax reforms for emissions of eight air pollutants: SOx compounds, NOx compounds, total suspended particulates (TSP's), particulate matter, volatile organic compounds (VOC's), carbon dioxide, carbon monoxide, and lead. The emissions factor approach relates emissions in given proportions to the uses of various inputs (usually fuel inputs) by industries. Emissions factors for a given pollutant can differ both by type of fuel and by the industry (or process) using the fuel. Thus, aggregate emissions of a given pollutant can change both as a result of changes in the input mix and from changes in the industry composition of aggregate output.

Ideally, one would like to connect changes in these emissions to changes in concentrations and changes in health and welfare. Outside the realm of greenhouse gases this is especially difficult, because many of these pollutants are locally concentrated. This means one needs a model with a spatial dimension, and the spatial detail may have to be quite fine.

5.3 RESULTS FROM A SAMPLING OF NUMERICAL MODELS

5.3.1 Results from the Goulder Model

Here I will briefly sketch results from simulations in which a fossil fuel Btu tax or a consumer gasoline tax increase is implemented in revenue-neutral fashion, with the revenues devoted to reductions in the income tax. I will only sketch the results - for a more detailed discussion, see Bovenberg and Goulder (1997).

An important item to keep in mind when interpreting the results is the relative taxation of capital land. In the baseline, or reference equilibrium (and under central values for parameters), the marginal excess burden of capital taxes is .43, while the MEB of labour taxes is .31. This means that the tax shifting effect works in favour of the second dividend when policies shift the burden of taxation from (overtaxed) capital to (undertaxed). In this regard, note that while the Btu tax tends to fall more or less evenly on capital and, the petroleum tax tends to fall mainly on labour (by virtue of its being akin to a consumption tax). Hence the gasoline tax has more potential for tax shifting that supports the second dividend.

Figure 5.1 shows results when these taxes are introduced with *lump sum* replacement of the revenues. Figure 1a shows that in the short term, the environmental (Btu and gas) taxes entail a greater GDP sacrifice than the personal income tax. Figure 1b shows that the gasoline tax has a much smaller investment cost than does the Btu tax or income tax. This reflects the fact that the gasoline tax tends to ease the tax burden on capital.

Table 5.1 shows the effects of these policies on factor prices and quantities. It indicates that the combination of petroleum tax increase and reduction in personal income tax reduces capital's tax burden and raises labour's. In contrast, the combination of Btu tax and a cut in personal income tax does not significantly alter the relative taxation of capital and labour.

Thus, the revenue neutral policy involving the petroleum tax produces a more significant tax shifting effect.

Table 5.2 shows welfare effects. These are the monetary equivalent (using the equivalent variation) of the change in utility associated with the policy change. These welfare measures disregard welfare impacts associated with the changes in environmental quality; they refer only to the cost side of the benefit-cost ledger.

Comparing the left and right columns indicates the importance of the revenue recycling effect; that is, of returning revenues through cuts in marginal tax rates instead of through lump sum tax cuts. The welfare costs of the revenue-neutral reforms are significantly higher when revenues are returned in lump sum fashion.

Concentrate now on the right column, which displays results from revenue-neutral policies in which the environmental tax revenues finance reductions in the personal tax. There are two main results from this column. First, the second dividend does not arise: the gross welfare costs (i.e., the costs before separating out the environmental benefits) are positive. Second, the welfare cost is lower for the petroleum tax reform, despite the narrower base of the petroleum tax. This reflects the tax shifting effect: as Table 5.1 indicated, under the petroleum tax reform the tax burden is shifted from capital to labour, which tends to reduce the gross costs. However, the tax-shifting effect is not strong enough to undo the cost associated with the tax interaction effect.

Is it possible to make the tax-shifting effect large enough to give the second dividend? Yes. The tax-shifting effect will be stronger to the extent that (1) the initial inefficiencies in the relative taxation of capital and labour are large, and (2) the policy shifts the burden from the overtaxed to the undertaxed factor. To enhance the first condition, we have performed simulations with very elastic capital supply assumptions. Specifically, we assume that the elasticity of substitution in consumption (which affects the household's interest elasticity of saving) is 'high' relative to most estimates. To enhance the second condition, we consider a policy in which a petroleum tax is introduced and all the revenues from this tax are recycled through cuts in capital taxes only. This combination produces a large enough tax shifting effect to yield the second dividend if the intertemporal elasticity of substitution is 1.8 or more. Although this shows that the second dividend can arise, producing this dividend seems to require implausibly high values for the intertemporal elasticity of substitution (most estimates are between 0 and unity[8]).

---

8 Using time-series data, Hall (1988) estimates that this elasticity is below 0.2. A cross-section analysis by Lawrance (1991) generates a central estimate of 1.1. Estimates from time-series tend to be lower than those from cross-section analyses.

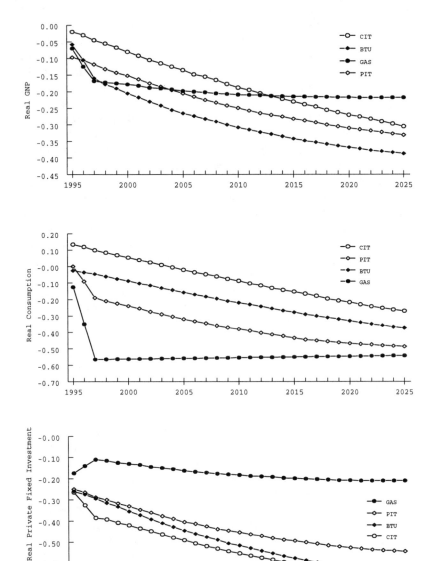

Figure 5.1 Aggregate effects of energy and income tax policies. Revenue replacement via lump sum tax cuts (percentage changes from reference case)

Table 5.1   Comparative numerical results

					Results		
					Welfare change	Pct. change in real GNP	
Model	Reference	Country	Type of environ-mental Tax	Form of revenue Replacement		pd. 1	pd. 21
DRI	Shackleton et al. (1992)	US	Phased-in Carbon Tax	Personal Tax Cut	-0.39	-0.00	-0.76
Goulder	Goulder (1994a)	US	$25/ton Carbon Tax	"	-0.33	-0.15	-0.22
"	Goulder (1994b)	US	Fossil Fuel Btu Tax	"	-0.28	-0.09	-0.18
Jorgenson - Wilcoxen	Shackleton et al. (1992)	US	Phased-in Carbon Tax	Labour Tax Cut	1.01	0.03	-0.41
"	"	US	"	Capital Tax Cut	0.19	0.20	0.95
LINK	"	US	"	Personal Tax Cut	-0.51	0.00	-0.35
Shah-Larsen	Shah & Larsen (1992)	US	$10/ton	"	-1049	-0.020	
"	"	India	"	"	-129	-0.060	
"	"	Indo-nesia	"	"	-4	-0.005	
"	"	Japan	"	"	-269	-0.008	
"	"	Paki-stan	"	"	-23	-0.070	

Table 5.2   Welfare impacts

	Welfare Cost Per Dollar of Revenue	
	Lump-Sum Tax Replacement	Personal Income Tax Replacement
BTU Tax	.656	.318
Consumer-Level Petroleum Tax Increase	.594	.253
Personal Income Tax Increase	.379	

5.3.2   Results from a Selection of Other Models

Table 5.3 summarizes results from numerical studies of a revenue-neutral carbon tax policy. The table presents results from seven numerical models. These are the Goulder and Jorgenson-Wilcoxen intertemporal general equilibrium models of the US, the Proost-Regemorter general equilibrium model of Belgium, the DRI and LINK econometric macroeconomic models of the US, and the Shah-Larsen partial equilibrium model, which has been applied to five countries, including the US.[9] The results in Table 5.3 are for the revenue-neutral combination of an environmental tax (usually a carbon tax) and reduction in the personal income tax, except in cases where this combination was not available.

All welfare changes abstract from changes in welfare associated with improvements in environmental quality (reductions in greenhouse gas emissions). Thus they correspond to the gross cost concept discussed above. In the Goulder, Jorgenson-Wilcoxen, and Proost-Regemorter models, welfare changes are reported in terms of the equivalent variation; in the Shah-Larsen model, the changes are based on the compensating variation.[10] In the DRI and LINK macroeconomic models, the percentage change in aggregate real consumption substitutes for a utility-based welfare measure.[11]

In most cases, the revenue-neutral green tax swap implies a reduction in welfare, that is, it entails positive gross costs. This militates against the double dividend claim. Results from the Jorgenson-Wilcoxen model, however, support the double dividend notion. Relatively high interest elasticities of savings (a high capital supply elasticity) and the assumption of perfect capital mobility across sectors may partially explain this result, at least in the case where revenues from the carbon tax are devoted to cuts in marginal taxes on capital. These assumptions imply large marginal excess burdens (MEBs) from taxes on capital, considerably larger than the MEBs from labour taxes. As indicated above, if the MEB on capital significantly

---

9   For a more detailed description of these models, see Goulder (1995b), Jorgenson and Wilcoxen (1990, 1996), Shackleton *et al.* (1996), Proost and Regemorter (1995), and Shah and Larsen (1992). The Shah-Larsen model is the simplest of the models, in part because it takes pre-tax factor prices as given. Despite its simplicity, the model addresses interactions between commodity and factor markets and thus incorporates some of the major efficiency connections discussed earlier.

10 The equivalent variation is the lump-sum change in wealth which, under the 'business-as-usual' or base case, would leave the household as well off as in the policy change case. Thus a positive equivalent variation indicates that the policy is welfare improving. The compensating variation is the lump sum change in wealth that, in the policy change scenario, would cause the household to be as well off as in the base case. In reporting the Shah-Larsen results we adopt the convention of multiplying the compensating variation by -1, so that a positive number in the table signifies a welfare improvement here as well.

11 The demand functions in these models are not derived from an explicit utility function. Hence they do not yield utility based measures.

Table 5.3 Numerical assessments of welfare impacts of revenue-neutral environmental tax reforms

Model	Welfare Reference	Country	Type of Environmental Tax	Method of Revenue Replacement	Effect
DRI	Shackleton et al. (1996)	US	Phased-in Carbon Tax[a]	Personal Tax Cut	-0.39[b]
Goulder	Goulder (1995b)	US	$25/ton Carbon Tax	Personal Tax Cut	-0.33[c]
"	Goulder (1994)	US	Fossil Fuel Btu Tax	Personal Tax Cut	-0.28[c]
Jorgenson-Wilcoxen	Shackleton et al. (1996)	US	Phased-in Carbon Tax[a]	Capital Tax Cut	0.19[d]
LINK	Shackleton et al. (1996)	US	Phased-in Carbon Tax[a]	Personal Tax Cut	-0.51[b]
MSE					
Proost-Regemorter	Proost and Regemorter (1995)	Belgium	Hybrid of Carbon and Energy Tax	Payroll (Social Security) Tax Cut	-3.45[d]
Shah-Larsen	Shah and Larsen (1992)	U.S.	$10/ton Carbon Tax	Personal Tax Cut	-1049[e]
"	"	India	"	"	-129
"	"	Indonesia	"	"	-4
"	"	Japan	"	"	-269
"	"	Pakistan	"	"	-23

Notes: (a) Beginning at $15/ton in 1990 (period 1), growing at five per cent annually to $39.80 per ton in 2010 (period 21), and remaining at that level thereafter. (b) Percentage change in the present value of consumption; the model does not allow for utility-based welfare measures. (c) Welfare cost per dollar of tax revenue, as measured by the equivalent variation. (d) Equivalent variation as a percentage of benchmark private wealth. (e) Compensating variation in levels (millions of US dollars).

exceeds that on labour, and the environmental reform shifts the tax burden onto labour, the double dividend can arise. Thus, the large MEBs from capital taxes help explain why, in the Jorgenson-Wilcoxen model, a revenue-neutral combination of carbon tax and reduction in capital taxes involves negative gross costs, that is, produces a double dividend.

Identifying the sources of differences in results across models is difficult, in large part because of the lack of relevant information on simulation outcomes and parameters. Relatively few studies have performed the type of analysis that exposes the channels underlying the overall impacts. There is a need for more systematic sensitivity analysis, as well as closer investigations of how structural aspects of tax policies (type of tax base, narrowness of tax base, uniformity of tax rates, etc.) influence the outcomes. In addition, key behavioural parameters need to be reported. Serious attention to these issues will help explain differences in results and, one hopes, lead to a greater consensus on likely policy impacts.

5.4   POLICY IMPLICATIONS AND PROMISING RESEARCH DIRECTIONS

5.4.1   Policy Implications

The theoretical and empirical results outlined above generate some important implications for green tax reform. Here are a few:

1. It is difficult to justify green tax reforms solely on the basis of the second dividend (a reduction in gross cost) or the third dividend (positive effects on employment). Numerical studies tend to support the analytical findings that the gross costs of revenue-neutral environmental tax reforms are positive. These tax interaction effects dominate the revenue recycling effect.
2. The absence of the second dividend does not imply that revenue neutral environmental tax reforms are misguided. Rather, it implies that to justify these reforms one must invoke the environmental benefits.
3. Because the tax-interaction effect outweighs the revenue recycling effect, the costs of environmental tax reforms are generallly higher in a second-best setting than in a first-best world. This implies that optimal environmental tax rate generally is less than the marginal environmental damages in a second-best setting with pre-existing factor taxes.[12]
4. Numerical results indicate that it makes a substantial difference whether revenues are returned lump sum or through cuts in distortionary taxes. Results from Bovenberg and Goulder (1996) indicate that if marginal benefits from carbon abatement are below $50 per ton, the optimal carbon tax is negative when revenues are returned lump sum. These results bear on the choice between alternative instruments for environmental protection - in particular, for the choice between emission taxes, on the one hand, and emission quotas or grandfathered emissions permits, on the other. Emissions taxes earn revenues and thus allow the possibility of exploiting the revenue recycling effect. In contrast, emission quotas or grandfathered emissions permits earn no revenue and do not offer opportunities to exploit

---

12 It should be less by a factor representing the marginal cost of public funds. In the Goulder model's representation of the US economy, the MCPF is not much different from unity (it is about 1.1), which implies that the optimal environmental tax rate in the second-best setting is about 90 per cent of the first-best optimal tax rate.

the revenue recycling effect. As shown by Parry (1996) and Goulder, Parry, and Burtraw (1997), the inability to exploit the revenue recycling effect puts this latter set of policies at a significant efficiency disadvantage relative to emission taxes. In this connection, Parry, Williams and Goulder (1997) show that the absence of the revenue recycling effect may imply that CO_2-abatement through carbon quotas or grandfathered carbon permits will be an efficiency-reducing proposition.

5. While the presence of tax shifting makes the second dividend a possibility, in practice it is difficult to generate the second dividend through tax shifting. To obtain the second dividend under a petroleum tax, one needs 'unusual' values for key parameters and revenue recycling needs to concentrate the tax relief toward capital.

5.4.2 Research Directions

We close with a brief list of research directions that seem particularly promising in light of the issues discussed earlier. In my view, recent theory has been extremely successful in clarifying the circumstances under which the different dividends from green tax reforms might arise. At the same time, the theory sometimes yields ambiguous results, especially in more complex models. In these cases, outcomes depend on model structure assumptions, functional forms, or parameter values. In these cases, there is great value to empirical work that helps refine our understanding of the key behavioural relationships or parameters. Here are some empirical efforts that might have especially large payoffs:

1. Closer attention to nature of household demands for commodities and for environmental quality. This would help indicate the extent to which the separability assumptions inherent in many analytical and numerical models might need to be relaxed. At issue is both the separability between consumer goods and leisure, and the separability between goods (including leisure) and environmental quality.
2. Further attention to the determinants and dynamics of capital and labour supply. This affects the efficiency costs of factor taxes and the potential scope of the tax-shifting effect.
3. Attention to the dynamics of nonrenewable resource supply. This could have an important bearing on the level and timing of revenues from environmental taxes and on the gross costs of these taxes.
4. Improved modelling of environmental benefits. Uncertainties will pervade every component of such modelling, but one hopes that, despite the uncertainties, the resulting models will yield useful information. Future assessments of green tax reforms might do well to indicate the extent of the uncertainties by giving results in terms of probability distributions. In the

context of global climate change policy, this information seems especially important. The key for a carbon tax is its ability to provide a degree of insurance against the low probability, high consequence outcome of very serious climate change. Models that consider only mean outcomes cannot account for this critical insurance function, and thus they will tend to understate the value of revenue-neutral carbon tax reforms.

In the past five years we have come a long way in our understanding of the economic impacts of green tax reforms. Theory casts doubt about the potential for the double (second) dividend. Nevertheless, even if the double dividend does not arise, there may be significant net benefits from green tax reforms, and much work needs to be done - especially empirical work - to get a better sense of the magnitudes of these net gains.

REFERENCES

Bovenberg, A. Lans and de Mooij, Ruud A. (1994), 'Environmental Levies and Distortionary Taxation', *American Economic Review* **84**, 1085-9.

Bovenberg, A. Lans and Goulder, Lawrence H. (1996), 'Optimal Environmental Taxation in the Presence of Other Taxes: General Equilibrium Analyses', *American Economic Review* **86**, 985-1000.

Bovenberg, A. Lans and Goulder, Lawrence H. (1997), 'Costs of Environmentally Motivated Taxes in the Presence of Other Taxes: General Equilibrium Analyses', *National Tax Journal*.

Bovenberg, A. Lans and Goulder, Lawrence H. (1998), 'Environmental Taxation', in A. Auerbach and M. Feldstein, (eds), *Handbook of Public Economics*, North-Holland, Second Edition, forthcoming.

Bovenberg, A. Lans and van der Ploeg, F. (1994), 'Environmental Policy, Public Finance and the Labour Market in a Second-Best World', *Journal of Public Economics*, **55**, 349-70.

Burniaux, J.-M., Martin, J.P., Nicoletti, G. and Oliveira-Martins, J. (1991), 'GREEN - A Multi-Region Dynamic General Equilibrium Model for Quantifying the Costs of Curbing CO_2 Emissions: A Technical Manual' OECD Department of Economics and Statistics Working Paper 104, Paris.

De Mooij, Ruud and Bovenberg, A. Lans (1997), 'Environmental Taxes, International Capital Mobility and Inefficient Tax Systems: Tax Burden vs. Tax Shifting', *International Tax and Public Finance,* **5**.

Goulder, Lawrence H. (1994), 'Energy Taxes: Traditional Efficiency Effects and Environmental Implications', in James M. Poterba (ed.), *Tax Policy and the Economy,* **8**, Cambridge, Mass., MIT Press.

Goulder, Lawrence H. (1995a), 'Environmental Taxation and the "Double Dividend": A Reader's Guide', *International Tax and Public Finance* **2**, 157-83.

Goulder, Lawrence H. (1995b), 'Effects of Carbon Taxes in an Economy with Prior Tax Distortions: An Intertemporal General Equilibrium Analysis', *Journal of Environmental Economics and Management*.

Goulder, Lawrence H., Parry, Ian W.H. and Burtraw, Dallas (1997), 'Revenue-Raising vs. Other Approaches to Environmental Protection: The Critical Significance of Pre-Existing Tax Distortions', *RAND Journal of Economics* **28**, 708-31.

Hall, Robert (1988), 'Intertemporal Substitution in Consumption', *Journal of Political Economy* **96**, 339-57.

Hudson, Edward and Jorgenson, Dale (1974), 'U.S. Energy Policy and Economic Growth, 1975-2000', *Bell Journal of Economics and Management Science,* **5**.

Jorgenson, Dale W. and Wilcoxen, Peter J. (1990), 'Environmental Regulation and U.S. Economic Growth', *RAND Journal of Economics,* **21**, 314-40.

Jorgenson, Dale W. and Wilcoxen, Peter J. (1996), 'Reducing U.S. Carbon Emissions: An Econometric General Equilibrium Assessment', in Darius Gaskins and John Weyant (eds), *Reducing Global Carbon Dioxide Emissions: Costs and Policy Options,* Energy Modeling Forum, Stanford University, Stanford, California.

Lawrance, Emily (1991), 'Poverty and the Rate of Time Preference: Evidence from Panel Data', *Journal of Political Economy* **99**, 54-77.

Parry, Ian W.H. (1995), 'Pollution Taxes and Revenue Recycling', *Journal of Environmental Economics and Management* **29**, 64-77.

Parry, Ian W.H. (1996), 'Environmental Taxes and Quotas in the Presence of Distorting Taxes in Factor Markets', *Resource and Energy Economics,* forthcoming.

Parry, Ian W.H., Williams III, Roberton C. and Goulder, Lawrence H. (1997), 'When Can Carbon Abatement Policies Increase Welfare?, The Fundamental Role of Distorted Factor Markets', Working paper, Resources for the Future, Washington, DC.

Proost, S. and van Regemorter, D. (1995), 'The Double Dividend and the Role of Inequality Aversion and Macroeconomic Regimes', *International Tax and Public Finance* **2**, August 1995.

Schob, Ronnie (1994), 'Environmental Review and Distortionary Taxation: Environmental View vs. Public Finance View', Discussion Paper No. 436, Department of Economics, University of Essex, November.

Shackleton, Robert, Shelby, Michael, Cristofaro, Alex, Brinner, Roger, Yanchar, Goulder, Lawrence, Jorgenson, Dale, Wilcoxen, Peter and Pauly, Peter (1996), 'The Efficiency Value of Carbon Tax Revenues', in Darius Gaskins and John Weyant, (eds), *Reducing Global Carbon Dioxide Emissions: Costs and Policy Options.* Stanford, California, Energy Modeling Forum.

Shah, Anwar and Larsen, Bjorn (1992), 'Carbon Taxes, the Greenhouse Effect and Developing Countries', World Bank Policy Research Working Paper Series No. 957, The World Bank, Washington, DC.

6 General Equilibrium Effects of Increasing Carbon Taxes in Sweden

Glenn W. Harrison and Bengt Kriström

Sweden was one of the first countries to introduce carbon taxes. Along with many other countries that are concerned with the risk of global warming, it is currently evaluating further carbon taxes. We were asked to advise a government Commission charged with undertaking the official Swedish evaluation. We did so by constructing and simulating a computable general equilibrium (CGE) model of Sweden.

We review the carbon tax debate in Sweden in Section 1. The model is described in Section 2, and the main results presented in Section 3.

6.1 THE CARBON TAX DEBATE IN SWEDEN

6.1.1 Climate Policy in Sweden

Sweden has signed the Rio Declaration, which means that the current goal is to stabilize CO_2 emissions at the 1990 level. Indeed, the 1991 carbon tax was introduced with this target in mind: to reduce Swedish emissions by the year 2000. Given that 1990 was a particularly 'mild' year for Sweden in terms of economic activity and carbon emissions, this goal is likely to be relatively difficult for Sweden to attain.

The most important issue of future energy policy in Sweden is the fate of nuclear power. The current interpretation of the 1980 referendum is that nuclear power should be abolished by 2010, a goal that may conflict with unilateral climate policy goals. The future of nuclear power in Sweden is therefore unclear. A Commission on Future Energy Policy has been reviewing the matter and reported in 1995. In essence it recommended *against* a complete shutdown in 2010, generating considerable debate in policy circles. Uncertainty about future energy policy may have induced the government to change its climate policy from an active unilateral policy to the vague, internationally cooperative, framework that currently dominates the political discussion in Sweden.

An important analysis of the costs of closing down nuclear power within a binding CO_2 constraint was carried out by Bergman (1991). His calculations, based on a small CGE model, suggested significant costs of closing nuclear power while stabilizing (or reducing) CO_2 emissions. Assuming freely mobile capital internationally, this model suggests a significant leakage of Swedish firms to lower cost countries. This leakage argument has also influenced the debate and may have been important in redirecting earlier CO_2 goals.

In summary, Sweden's climate policy is mainly affected by three issues. The first is the concern for the international competitiveness of energy-intensive industry. We discuss below how this concern has been mapped into various exemptions and deductions. The second is the awareness of the link between nuclear power and CO_2 emissions, which we evaluate later. The third is the new emphasis on international cooperation, the entrance into the EU being the most dramatic example.

6.1.2 The Remit of the 'Green Tax' Commission

In March 1995 the Swedish government launched a Commission to provide an analysis of a tax system intended to have a stronger environmental profile. The Commission was asked to evaluate prevailing environmental taxes, and to scrutinize the potential for a 'double dividend' from new carbon taxes. The terms of reference include scrutiny of impacts on labour markets, the budget effects, 'competitiveness', dynamic impacts, distributional impacts, environmental aspects, as well as an analysis of the administrative properties of any proposal the Commission might want to put forward.

In the economics literature the 'double dividend' argument has come to circle around revenue-neutral substitution between labour and environmental taxes.[1] While there certainly exists other sets of taxes with the appropriate mix of distortionary impacts, the discussion within the Commission and in the academic literature focuses mainly on energy-labour tax substitutions.

Because Sweden is a small open economy, it is also important to look at the impact of a tax-swap on international 'competitiveness'. The Commission should describe the effects of its proposals on the environment and detail the distributional impacts of the reform. Finally, the Commission should also map out the potential environmental gains of the eventual reform.

6.1.3 The General Structure of Swedish Energy Taxes

Sweden has used taxes on energy since 1929, when a tax on petroleum was introduced. Electricity has been taxed since 1951, followed by a broadening of the energy taxes in 1957. The motivation underlying these taxes was purely

---

1   See Goulder (1995a) for a review.

financial. In the 1970s, propelled by the global energy crisis, energy taxes were increasingly motivated by a desire to discourage consumption of fossil fuels. Thus, increased taxes on oil products were coupled by a significant expansion of electricity supply in order to promote a different profile of energy consumption.

Environmental concerns entered the discussion in the 1980s, manifested by the introduction of a tax differentiation of leaded petroleum in 1986. This was followed by the Environmental Tax Commission that recommended a rich array of environmental taxes in their final proposal (see SOU 1990:59). This investigation led the government to propose taxes on emissions of CO_2 and sulphur, *inter alia*, in 1991. While this was not the first official body in Sweden to discuss environmental taxes, this mission was unique in that it was coupled with a major overhaul of the Swedish tax system in the beginning of the 1990s. The general tax reform included a reduction of income taxes, to be financed partially by an increased use of energy and environmental taxes (including the introduction of VAT on energy consumption).[2]

For the purpose of harmonizing Swedish energy taxes with those prevalent within the most important competing countries, another reform of energy taxation was passed on 1 January, 1993. This reform was closely tied with the international competitiveness concerns that have been a recurring issue in the design of Swedish energy policy. It meant that manufacturing industry no longer paid energy tax on the use of fuels and electricity in their processes. In addition, there was a reduction in the CO_2 tax for the manufacturing industry, as detailed below.

A. Industry Exemptions

In an international context Swedish energy taxes are high. Because export-oriented industries are competing in markets with significant price elasticities, it is not surprising that several tax exemptions are being used. Beginning in 1974, through the law on (partial) exemptions of the general energy tax, energy-intensive manufacturing industries and the horticulture industry have escaped some part of energy taxes. This, of course, is not unique in Europe. Similar exemptions have also been used in Denmark and Norway for manufacturing.

These exemptions for manufacturing are a key feature of the tax system we evaluate. In the tax system prior to 1993 approximately 100 energy-intensive firms were granted reduced tax rates on fuels and electricity. In 1992 the reduction for energy-intensive industry was worth 1.3 billion SEK. The new

---

2 Of the total change in tax revenues, estimated at about 90 billion SEK, energy and environmental taxes were estimated to generate 3 billion SEK in the absence of changes in the VAT treatment of energy. The addition of VAT on energy added another estimated 14 billion SEK in revenue (Åke Nordlander, personal communication).

energy and carbon tax system introduced in 1993 resulted in significantly reduced tax rates for industry. The total amount of energy and carbon tax collections dropped from 3.8 billion SEK in 1992 to just 0.5 billion SEK in
1994. We approximate these exemptions as applying to manufacturing industries *in toto*, so that manufacturing industry and horticulture are assumed to
pay 25 per cent of the general carbon tax rate.

Before the 1993 change of the energy tax system, tax exemptions were
essentially granted on a case-by-case basis. Thus energy-intensive industries
could apply for a reduction of the energy tax on electricity and fuels. With a
zero energy tax on electricity and fossil fuels, such applications are now
redundant. There are still possibilities for deductions for fuel use, some of
them of considerable importance for individual firms (see SOU (1994:85; p.
106)). These deductions are only possible for firms producing cement, lignite
and glass, they only apply to the carbon tax on coal and natural gas, and not
on the use of oil products. In 1995 less than 10 energy-intensive firms could
benefit from this rule, and the value of the reduced tax was less than 50
million SEK.

B. The Carbon Dioxide Tax

By far the most important of the environmental taxes introduced as the result
of the Environmental Tax Commission is the carbon dioxide tax. Introduced
in January 1991, the tax of 0.25 SEK per kilogram of emitted CO_2 was followed by intense controversy. Eventually, a reform of energy taxes in 1993
led to significant reductions for manufacturing industries, as explained above.
The government argued that it was important to reduce Swedish energy taxes
to European levels for internationally competitive industries, lest firms move
abroad or remain at a significant cost disadvantage. Carbon taxes in Sweden
in 1995, the base year of the model's representation of the tax system, are
generally about 0.34 SEK per kilogram of emitted CO_2 for non-exempted
sectors and 0.083 SEK per kilogram for manufacturing sectors.

6.1.4   The European Union

An advisory referendum held in Sweden in November 1994 resulted in a 52-
47 per cent win for the proponents of entering the EU. As a result Sweden has
been a member of the EU since January 1995. It is not currently clear what
kinds of restrictions there will be on the possibilities of pursuing an independent environmental policy. On the one hand, current EU policy is based
on minimum requirements, which means that a member country has an option
to use a stricter policy. On the other hand, it is difficult to block imports of
goods that have been approved in another country. Membership of the EU

does not prevent country-specific environmental policies *de jure*, but it may make a deviation from EU policy impossible *de facto*.

When Sweden entered the EU a new energy tax law (SOU 1994:1776) replaced the old one. It replaced laws on general energy taxes, CO_2 taxes, sulphur taxes, petroleum taxes and diesel taxes. The new law substantially harmonizes Swedish rules with those in the EU. Generally, the above taxes are due on fuels used for heating purposes, or as propellants for engines. Biofuels are exempt from energy taxes, following a long tradition in Swedish energy policy to encourage substitution towards these fuels. Fossil fuels and electricity used in manufacturing are treated favourably, the motivation again being the concern with international competitiveness.

Current Swedish energy taxes generated about 40 billion SEK in 1994. The structure of these revenues, in terms of the CO_2 tax and other energy taxes, are shown in Figure 1. The total revenues from energy and environmental taxes in 1994, including sales taxes on motor vehicles and annual road taxes, were roughly 47 billion SEK (Treasury of Sweden (1995; p. 60)). This corresponds to about 6 per cent of total tax revenues (Treasury of Sweden (1995; Fig 13.1, p. 61)) or about 3 per cent of GDP.

6.2 A GENERAL EQUILIBRIUM MODEL

6.2.1 Basic Features

Our Small Open Economy (SOE) model is designed for tax policy analysis with a large number of sectors. The model is a 'generic' general equilibrium model of a single economy along the lines of Melo and Tarr (1992), Harrison, Rutherford and Tarr (1993) and Rutherford, Rutström and Tarr (1994). We describe here the general features of the base model, adding details about the 1992 version for Sweden later. Further details on the database construction are provided in Harrison and Kriström (1996; Appendix A). The complete database and model is available in machine-readable form from web page http://theweb.badm.sc.edu/glenn/sweden.htm.

Goods are produced using primary factors and intermediate inputs. Primary factors include capital and six types of labour. Production exhibits constant returns to scale and individual firms behave competitively, selecting output levels such that marginal cost at those output levels equals the given market price. Output is differentiated between goods destined for the domestic and export markets. Exports are further distinguished according to whether they are destined for specific foreign markets. This relationship is characterized by a two-level constant elasticity of a transformation frontier. Composite output is an aggregate of domestic output and composite exports; composite exports are aggregates of exports for distinct foreign markets.

Final demand by private households arises from nested constant elasticity of substitution (CES) utility functions. This allows consumer decision making to occur in the form of multi-stage budgeting. At the top level goods from different sectors compete subject to the budget constraint of the consumer, and all income elasticities are united. In the second stage the consumer decides how much to spend on domestic or imported goods in each sector, subject to income allocated to spending in that sector in the first stage. Finally, having decided how much to spend on imports as a whole, the consumer allocates this expenditure on imports from specific countries. Each allocation decision is modelled as a CES function.

The model allows tariff rates to differ depending on whether the imports are from specific trading partners. Exports can be sold at different prices depending on whether they are destined for distinct foreign markets. The same is possible on the import side.

Government expenditures and investment demand are exogenous. Funding of government expenditures is provided by tax revenues and tariff revenues. In addition to tariffs, the government also derives income from indirect taxes (net of subsidies). These are modelled as Value Added Taxes (VAT). Unless otherwise specified the government recovers any lost revenues by increasing taxes on labour collected at the enterprise level; similarly, it reduces those taxes for any increase in revenue due to a counter-factual scenario.

Since private consumption equals the income from primary factors plus net transfers to the consumer by the government (from domestic and foreign trade taxes), Walras law is satisfied. Public consumption is balanced with revenue.

World market import and export prices are fixed, so there are no endogenous changes in the terms of trade. In other words, import supplies and export demands are infinitely elastic at given world prices. The current account balances the value of exports and imports taking into account exogenously-fixed capital inflows. Our model allows for changes in these fixed world prices.

6.2.2   The Swedish Model

Based on 1992 input-output data for Sweden, the model identifies 87 sectors.[3] These are listed in Table 6.1, along with their pseudo-Swedish acronym. This is the level of disaggregation available through the input-output statistics, and provides excellent detail for our purposes. It is possible to aggregate to a smaller number of sectors, such as has been popular in previous CGE models of Sweden, but there seems little advantage in doing so and potential for mis-

---

3 The input-output database formally identifies 88 sectors, but one of these is effectively a 'dummy' sub-industry which contains no transactions and is therefore deleted. We therefore refer to the model as having 87 sectors.

leading analysis in the present context.[4] Moreover, it is always possible to assess the information loss of employing specific aggregations if the model is fully disaggregated, while the reverse is obviously not true.

The household disaggregation is based on the 1992 Household Expenditure Survey conducted by the 'Statistiska Centralbyrån' (SCB). It provides detailed information on expenditure patterns of 30 households. These households are differentiated by family status and income, and are listed along with their acronyms in Table 6.2. One difficulty is that the expenditures of each household are defined over consumer goods, and no ready mapping exists from our industrial products to those goods. We resolve this problem by using our intuition, and using the data from the household expenditure survey to allow different households to have different expenditure patterns for different industrial goods.

We also assume that each household receives it's income from slightly different sources. In other words, each household has a slightly different *share* of each primary factors in its endowment. In the absence of better data, we are not overly confident of this feature of the model, and prefer to view households as being primarily distinguished on the basis of their expenditure patterns. Hence we primarily capture variations in the cost of living for different households, and probably do not capture all of the variations in the value of endowment income for different households.

Primary factors are used in the production of value added in each sector. In general two types of factors are free to move across sectors to equate after-tax rates of return: labour and capital (K). Labour is differentiated by skill categories and occupational status into six groups: blue-collar unskilled (L_BC_U), blue-collar skilled (L_BC_S), white-collar unskilled (L_WC_U), white-collar semi-skilled (L_WC_SS), white-collar skilled (L_WC_S) and

---

4 The primary argument for aggregation, given the ready availability of powerful software and hardware for these models, has to do with the 'reliability' of data and priors at the proposed level of aggregation. Several of the data items required for our analysis are only available at an aggregated level, although far fewer than one would think and still at a relatively disaggregated level of about 20 or 30 sectors. Harrison and Kriström (1996; Appendix A) documents our data collation efforts, and the instances where we needed to map one aggregate sector into several of our disaggregated sectors. For example, basic data on factor payments were generally available only at the 3-digit SNR level, while our full model employs many 4-digit sectors. Hence we needed to use the former as the basis for individual sectors at the latter level of disaggregation. With respect to the use of *a priori* judgements, our belief is that it is much easier to apply serious priors to detailed sectors than it is to synthetic aggregates. In any event, if the priors in question are essentially held in a diffuse manner over a range of sectors, then nothing is lost if one so applies them in our disaggregated model. Providing the reader knows when such uniform assumptions are being applied, and is not dazzled by the fake detail of the analysis, it is foolish to 'hardwire' in the level of application of priors by aggregation. Formal decision-theoretic methods of aggregation of input-output sectors are explored by Harrison and Manning (1976) and provide statistically informative alternatives to naïve aggregation as practiced by many early-generation CGE modellers. However, sophisticated or naïve aggregation is simply misplaced in the present setting.

employed (L_SE). The per cent distribution of labour types in each sector is shown in Table 6.6. We allow the labour types to substitute with each other at a different rate than their composite does with K, although our formulation allows all primary factors to be equally substitutable as a special case.[5]

The model allows the specification of sector-specific capital types in any set of sectors. This possibility allows the identification of sectors that employ a significant amount of a primary factor that can be interpreted as specific to that sector. We could interpret this as referring to some 'short run' in which capital is applied to sectors in a manner that does not permit it to be readily moved to other sectors.[6] Instead, we use it to capture the limited range of activities to which resources can be applied. As one increases parametrically the assumed share of benchmark payments to K that are attributable to such factors, the corresponding supply curve for that industry becomes more inelastic. The intuition is clear: as the relative demand for output for that industry falls, *ceteris paribus* all input prices, the factor that is specific to this industry cannot escape to other sectors. It must therefore experience a larger drop in real return than when it is inter-sectorally mobile and facing the same drop in derived demand for its value marginal product. This relatively sharp decline in factor input cost results in a larger drop in the supply price in that industry than when the factor is assumed mobile. The converse argument applies to increases in demand in the industry, of course. Thus we can arbitrarily constrain the supply response of resource-based industries by specification of this parameter.[7] Given that the primary policy focus of these simulations is on the use of fossil fuels, such assumptions may be important.

Each sector produces output using intermediate inputs and a value added composite of the primary factors. Although the natural assumption might be to model the substitutability of the intermediate inputs by assuming a Leontief technology[8], we use instead a CES function with a low elasticity of substitu-

---

5   This formulation employs a nested production function in which K and composite labour substitute at the 'top level' to produce value added in a given sector. At the 'bottom level' the labour types then substitute to produce the composite labour factor. Both levels are CES, hence setting the elasticities of substitution at each level to the same value results in the nests 'collapsing' into one level in which the three substitute at that rate.

6   It is common to assume in the 'short run' that factors are likely to be sector-specific, and in the 'long-run' that factors tend to be mobile across sectors. We would expect a short run model of his kind to generate smaller welfare gains from a 'first-best' liberalization, since resources are constrained in their ability to reallocate to more productive uses. On the other hand, we would expect the short run model to exhibit less extreme changes in production structure since the sector-specificity of factors generates less elastic supply schedules. We also recognize that some factors are likely to be specific to one or other sectors even in the long run. An obvious example might be the natural resources used in mining.

7   Although we do not offer a detailed model of the rigidities in the oil and extraction sectors, this feature of our model is similar in effect to the model used in Bovenberg and Goulder (1995; fn.15).

8   Since the matter continues to be confused by commentators that should know better (e.g., Jorgenson and Wilcoxen (1995; p.176)), we stress that the assumption of a Leontief

tion (0.25) across all sectors. This specification allows for later evaluation of the effects of varying degrees of substitutability at the point at which energy taxes typically impact in Sweden. The value added composite is produced using a CES production function and consists of two inputs: a labour composite and a capital composite. Each of these composites, in turn, is produced in a lower CES nest.

Trade is modelled as occurring at fixed world prices. However, Swedish importers may substitute between alternative import sources, and indeed between domestic production and an import composite. Similar assumptions apply on the export side, where Swedish producers have a constant elasticity of transformation between (a) sales to domestic markets and a composite foreign market, and (b) sales of the composite export to any of several foreign trading partners. The key feature of our model in these regards is that Swedish producers have no market power in world markets.

In the present version we identify trade with Finland, Norway, Denmark, the rest of the EU, Japan, the United States, and a residual Rest of World (ROW). Hence there are 7 trading partners in the model. No data is available to identify different tariff rates or NTB policies for any trading partner, so we assume that the trade distortions applying in aggregate (estimated from the input-output data) apply in a non-discriminatory fashion to all importers. We could extend this to allow for the discriminatory rates applying to EU member countries following Sweden's recent accession to the EU.

The specification of energy and carbon taxes are central to the model. To capture their structure, particularly with respect to the use of sectoral exemptions, we model them as falling on trade in intermediate inputs. This allows us considerable flexibility to calibrate the model precisely to capture the distortionary effects of existing taxes at the correct margin in terms of our model. Table 6.3 lists the estimates we have generated of the carbon taxes applicable in Sweden in 1995, and Table 6.4 lists the estimates for energy and sulphur taxes. These rates are displayed as follows: each column shows the good whose use as an *input* in the production of the row good generates the percentage tax liability indicated.[9] Thus, for example, production in sector JORD uses intermediate inputs from sector PETR and effectively incurs an *ad*

---

technology is not mandated by our use of the calibration approach to estimation, nor by computational constraints. In general we do restrict ourselves to nested-CES functions, although they can be used to represent globally regular functional forms in a locally flexible manner (see Perroni and Rutherford (1995a, 1995b)).

9   The rates are defined legally as relying on the use of one of several primary energy types. We estimate the physical usage of each energy type in each sector, then estimate the value of the usage of each energy type in each sector by applying average 1995 prices for each type, and then infer value of carbon (sulphur) taxes paid by each sector on its use of each energy type. We then aggregate these inferred tax payments, aggregate the payments for the use of energy by that sector, and calculate an *ad valorem* carbon tax on a net basis. These calculations allow us to generate carbon tax estimates for each sector that properly reflect the primary energy usage of each sector.

valorem carbon tax of 64 per cent on those inputs. Similarly, sector JORD uses inputs from sector GASV and pays instead an effective carbon tax of 61 per cent. These estimates take into account the partial exemptions for manufacturing sectors applicable for carbon taxes in 1995. The energy and sulphur taxes should be read the same way.

Information on value added taxes, social security taxes on labour, capital taxes, import tariffs, production taxes (other than energy or pollution taxes), and production subsidies are assembled from various sources described in Harrison and Kriström (1996; Appendix A). The rates assumed for the value added taxes and factor taxes reflect statutory rates applicable in 1995, and the other rates reflect actual collections as documented in the Input-Output table for 1992. Although these pre-existing distortions are all incorporated at a detailed sectoral level, in many cases the sectoral variations are small. This feature of the model could be improved with additional work on the background data, and would likely result in more substantial 'second-best' effects from the carbon tax scenarios considered later.

Estimates of elasticities of substitution must be assumed for primary factor substitution, value added and intermediate input substitution, import demand, detailed import components, import source, and domestic demand; elasticities of transformation must also be assumed for the allocation of domestic supply into domestic and exported markets, the allocation of exports into detailed export components, and the allocation of exports to destination. Despite our literature search, there are many elasticities about which there is considerable uncertainty. Our solution for that problem is to undertake a systematic sensitivity analysis in Harrison and Kriström (1996) with respect to key elasticities. Harrison and Vinod (1992), Harrison, Jones, Kimbell and Wigle (1993) and Harrison, Rutherford and Tarr (1993) demonstrate the role of systematic sensitivity analysis of models such as these with respect to plausible ranges of uncertainty about key elasticities.

The trade elasticities assumed in the model are particularly important. Higher trade elasticities tend to result in greater substitution away from energy-intensive sectors in Swedish production, as untaxed foreign production is substituted for taxed domestic production. We therefore use trade elasticities that reflect the best econometric estimates currently available (Reinert and Roland-Holst (1992) and Reinert and Shiells (1991)). Although they are low in relation to elasticity estimates used in some modelling exercises (e.g., Harrison, Rutherford and Tarr (1995, 1996)), it is important to stress that they are (a) based on explicit econometric estimates, and (b) used in a model that rules out any 'terms of trade effects' by assumption.[10]

---

10 The popular reason for using higher trade elasticities is that one can thereby avoid these effects, which are deemed unlikely *a priori* for a country as small in international trade terms as Sweden. Although the specification of trade elasticities that mitigate these effects is more involved than just assuming 'large' or 'small' values (e.g., see Harrison, Rutherford and Tarr

Estimates of carbon emissions in each sector were derived on the basis of information on physical usage of primary energy inputs. These data can then be used to infer the amount of carbon dioxide generated by each sector, since emissions are a reliable multiple of the physical amount of primary energy used. These estimates are listed in Table 6.7 for each sector, and reveal a familiar structure of the 'carbon economy'. The biggest emissions in aggregate terms come from SAMF (transport), EL_O (electricity generation), and the iron and steel complex (sectors JRN_, FERR, JNGJ, META, METV, and I_JA). Between them these sectors account for 71 per cent of total domestic emissions.

Another measure of the 'dirtiness' of a sector can be obtained by the level of carbon emissions for each million SEK of output it produces. By this measure the iron and steel complex comes off much worse than the transport and electricity sectors, generally by an order of magnitude. Although unimportant in terms of overall emissions, the TRAF (fibreboard) sector also has an extremely high emission relative to the value of its output.

Comparing the estimates of carbon taxes and the estimates of carbon emissions, the absence of taxes on the iron and steel complex is immediate. The formal reason for this is that these sectors are exempt. The stated rationale underlying this exemption is that they are particularly vulnerable to foreign competition and would be unable to 'pass on' any taxes on one of their inputs unless their competitors also bore comparable taxes.

Another feature of this comparison of sectoral carbon taxes and sectoral emissions is that, of the two biggest aggregate emitters, only EL_O pays the big tax on inputs of coal (output from sector STEN). Thus one could imagine the incentive within that sector to move away from coal-fired generators as the result of scalar increases in carbon taxes. This margin of choice is incorporated in the model, to the extent that sector EL_O can substitute away from intermediate inputs of STEN and towards PETR (or, to a lesser extent, GASV and SMOR).[11] The current version of the model adopts a CES production technology with respect to intermediate inputs, and assumes an elasticity of substitution of 0.25. It would obviously be useful to consider richer specifications of the energy technology in sector EL_O in future work.

The SOE model is generated with the GAMS/MPSGE software developed by Brooke, Kendrick and Meeraus (1992) and Rutherford (1992, 1995). It is then solved using the MILES algorithm developed by Rutherford (1993) or the PATH algorithm developed by Dirkse and Ferris (1995). Harrison and Kriström (1996; Appendix B) documents the computer software in some detail. Each scenario is typically solved in less than a minute on a Pentium-based personal computer running at 90mhz with at least 16mb RAM.

(1996)), these are not debates which are relevant here.

11 It should be noted that the STEN sector also has some oil importing activity, all of which is sold to the PETR sector.

6.3   EFFECTS OF CARBON TAX POLICIES

6.3.1   Baseline Policies and Simulation Scenarios

Table 6.5 lists the simulations we report here. The core simulation, which we then interpret with the other simulations, is called C100 and involves a 100 per cent increase in existing carbon taxes in Sweden. As a default we lower labour taxes so as to ensure equal government revenue after the carbon tax policy. Thus C100 incorporates the existing structure of carbon taxes, in particular the current exemptions.

We study the effects of alternative revenue replacement tax instruments with simulations C100V and C100LS. The first uses the VAT, and the second uses lump-sum taxes as a replacement device. Lump-sum taxes are levied on each household in proportion to their benchmark income, but are otherwise a lump-sum.

The effects of politically-imposed constraints on nuclear power plants are studied in the N100 and N75 simulations. In each case we assume the same basic scenario as the core simulation, C100, but impose a constraint that the physical output of the Electricity sector (EL_O) be maintained at no more than 100 or 75 per cent of the benchmark level. Since nuclear-generated power represents roughly 50 per cent of existing electricity in Sweden, these constraints are a plausible representation of the partial effects of maintaining the proposed ban on nuclear power. This constraint is complementary slack in the model to a tax on the electricity sector, such that if the constraint is violated then the sector is taxed until it reduces output and meets the constraint. It is expected that this constraint will significantly increase the welfare cost of the carbon tax increase, as consumers and industry face higher electricity prices. The model incorporates all of the general equilibrium effects of the tax on electricity required to meet the constraint.

6.3.2   Effects of Expanding the Carbon Tax

A. Welfare Impacts

The detailed welfare impacts of the C100 scenario are presented in Table 6.8. The first column lists the acronym of the household, defined in Table 6.2. The second and third columns report the percentage share of each household type in the total population of households or individuals.[12] We can use households

---

12 We do not distinguish vertically-challenged individuals (children) from the rest. If one wants to do so, then the use of household shares as a proxy has the unfortunate implication of unduly penalizing multiple-individual households. It would be possible to make some plausible inferences about the number of children in each of our household groups, given the way that they are defined, but we see no logic in disenfranchising those that happen to be politically disenfranchised by current voting entitlements.

or individuals as the bases of alternate social welfare function. Using individuals has the effect, relative to using households, of giving the 'single person' household groups a lower weight in social welfare, and enhances the weight of those households with more children.

The fourth column reports the value of the utility index for each household, normalized without loss of generality to 100 in the benchmark. Thus a value of 99.7 in this column indicates that the household type has experienced a decrease in the utility index of 0.3 per cent. A more meaningful evaluation is provided in the final two columns, which list the equivalent variation (EV) in income needed to make the individual or household as well off as they are in the new counter-factual equilibrium (evaluated at benchmark prices).

The EV is positive for welfare gains from the counter-factual policy scenario, and negative for losses. We report it in terms of SEK over a one-year period for *each individual in the household group* or for *each household in the household group*. Thus these values can be interpreted as the minimum amount of money that each individual or household in each household group would need to have received, if the policy or scenario had not occurred, for them to just as well off as if it had occurred. It is important to note that this welfare evaluation takes no account of the direct benefits to the household of the resulting reduction in aggregate emissions of either pollutant. Thus we can view these estimates as indicators of the minimum benefits which each consumer would have to perceive from the reduction in pollution in order for that consumer to regard the policy as a good one from an individual perspective.

In the C100 scenario we can therefore see that all household groups *lose* from a doubling of the existing carbon tax. For the single-adult household the cost is relatively modest, and well below the cognitive threshold value of 500 SEK. The costs become more substantial for all other *households*, especially those with children. Married households with no children experience slightly higher costs than single households with no children. In general richer households within any group tend to bear higher costs, reflecting the greater carbon-intensity of their expenditure patterns and their higher initial incomes.[13]

There is an intriguing effect of having extra children on the costs of the carbon tax increase for households. Having one or two children tends to raise the cost to a married household. But having three or more children actually reduces the household cost. The puzzle is resolved by examining how expenditure patterns change with extra children, not to mention some introspection.[14] Having children implies that households must use consumption

---

13 The welfare changes are measured in terms of income-equivalents expressed in SEK per year. These income values are derived by applying the percentage change in utility to the benchmark income level of the household. If the percentage changes in utility are the same across households then richer households will have a larger income change due solely to their larger base incomes in SEK.

14 By the first author.

technologies that have a significant fixed cost component: the purchase of durables such as prams and toys. These tend to be more carbon-intensive than the variable cost component of having children (i.e., toys actually have more embodied carbon-content than diapers), and it is the variable cost component that plays more of a role for the second child since the fixed cost expenditures do not have to be as large. The effect from having more than one child appears to be due to an increase in the share of household expenditures being allocated to transport. Presumably this reflects the need to take more family holidays, or the effects of re-location decisions as households tend to move out of dense (and carbon-efficient) urban transportation networks into suburban transportation networks.[15]

The costs of the carbon tax increase is greatest for households that are married with two children, and for richer households. The 'other households' group also tends to bear a relatively high burden; this group consists mainly of children above the age of 17 living at home with their parents.[16] These households experience losses that are generally greater than 1000 SEK per year, and in several cases are more than 2500 SEK per year.

To repeat an important point, the fact that all households experience a loss does *not* mean that they would not benefit overall from the carbon tax increase. The reason is that we have neglected the direct benefit they would reap from the reduction in aggregate carbon emissions that would (presumably) result from the policy. In fact our model estimates that there would be a reduction of carbon dioxide of 52 Ktons, as discussed later.[17] Although this is a modest reduction in per cent terms, it is *possible* that household M_2C_4 would value it at more than the 3033 SEK per year that would be the cost to that household to bring about the reduction. In the absence of any formal attempt to estimate the direct benefits to Swedish households from carbon reductions of various magnitudes, such judgements will have to be made politically. We provide some guidance on this matter later, but do not pretend that we know what these gross benefits are.

It should also be added that different households might have very different perceptions of the direct benefits of carbon reductions. Hence it could be the case that household M_2C_4 does get a benefit that exceed the 'price' it pays of 3033 SEK, but that household S_NC_2 does *not* get a benefit that exceeds the more modest 'price' of 283 SEK which it must pay. The gross benefits of any given commodity, whether it be 'stor stark öl' or '52 less Ktons of carbon on the planet,' can vary from household to household and individual to indi-

---

15 These speculations are supported by inspection of the differences across household expenditure shares that are 'driving' these results in our model, but is not modelled formally as a household technology with these scale effects.

16 The other groups, 'single' and 'cohabiting' households, only include one or two adults, respectively.

17 The term 'Ktons' refers to one *thousand* tons.

vidual. Indeed, it is plausible that having more children would make one more concerned about the quality of the environment in the future, and increase one's willingness to pay for carbon reductions. On the other hand, having children may also increase your discount rate, such that the enhanced benefits of carbon reduction in the future are insufficient to offset the enhanced 'price tag' to be paid now.

This is not to say that our estimates of welfare costs are worthless, but simply to identify the many factors which must be considered before they can be properly used to guide decision making. Implicit or explicit estimates of discount rates and gross benefits from carbon reductions must be made before an overall assessment of the C100 policy is possible. We stress these considerations since we will generally proceed to ignore them when describing the results.

There are several ways to 'aggregate' these detailed welfare impacts. The first is to just add up the EV values for all households, ignoring the distributional impact. In effect this represents the evaluation one gets from a simple utilitarian social welfare function (SWF). This type of SWF ignores who gains and loses, and only focuses on whether the aggregate pie has increased or not. In the present case it has clearly decreased, and the aggregate loss in income is 4 *billion* SEK per year. This aggregate is obtained by adding up the EV values in either of the last two columns of Table 6.8, multiplying each by the number of individuals or households in the household type as appropriate. It openly ignores the distributional burden of the welfare impacts.

Another way in which the overall impact of the C100 policy could be viewed is that it is the *aggregate* 'price tag' for the Swedish economy of a reduction in emissions of 52 Ktons of CO_2. A social counterpart to the more complete cost-benefit calculus described above for each individual household could now be undertaken. Such a calculus would require an estimate of the aggregate social benefits to Sweden of this reduction in physical emissions, perhaps by some official body such as the Green Tax Commission. This calculation would again entail the implicit or explicit use of a discount rate, in this case the social discount rate.

B. Emissions Impacts

How did we arrive at the estimate that a reduction of 52 Ktons of CO_2 would result from the C100 policy? The sectoral impact shown in Table 6.9 shows how these estimates were arrived at. Consider the last three columns, which show the aggregate change in physical emissions of CO_2 attributable to each sector.

The first of the three columns, marked CO2_D, shows the change due to changes in *domestic* production in that sector brought about by the C100 scenario. Thus we see that a reduction in domestic production of the STEN sector, indicated by a 6 per cent reduction in the value of domestic value added in column VA%, led to a reduction in physical emissions from that sector of 5 Ktons.

The fact that some sectors expand when there is an increase in carbon taxes is exactly what one would expect from a general economic equilibrium. The doubling of the carbon tax changes *relative* prices against the *most* carbon-intensive activities. The cheapest way for some industries to contract their use of the (intermediate) inputs of these carbon-intensive sectors *may* be to substitute towards the use of the products of other sectors that, while less carbon intensive than the ones they displace, might still be more carbon intensive than average for the economy as a whole. Why don't they substitute towards the products that are least carbon-intensive? Simple: their existing technology may not call for them to be used at all. So, even if they have the best relative price ratio because of the carbon tax rise, the value of their marginal product (as inputs) is still virtually zero.

For example, the DRYC sector is a wonderful sector, justifiably patronized by many Swedes. It also has a relatively low (direct) carbon intensity of only 3 Ktons of carbon per billion SEK of output. But when some sector such as JORD are contemplating increased prices for all modes of industrial transportation, sectors RALS, BILA and FLYG in our model, it cannot 'turn to DRYC' despite the temptation. It must re-allocate amongst these three transportation sectors, and in fact such decisions tend to go against RALS and in favour of the other two. The common sense reason that DRYC does not get the vote is that it has nothing technologically to do with reality-based transportation. The formal counterpart of this sobering intuition in our model is that the JORD sector has virtually no (direct) inputs of DRYC in the benchmark year of our Input-Output table, but it has substantial inputs of all three of the transportation inputs. Hence, by Marshall's second law of derived demand[18] the elasticity of demand for the alternative transport inputs will be relatively large and we can expect to see some net substitution effects there. Conversely, the elasticity of demand for DRYC will be relatively low, so we will not see any changes in the derived demand for it, despite it having a relatively favourable price ratio compared to transport inputs.

Turning now to the next to last column in Table 6.9, CO2_F, we see the effect of the Swedish policy on *foreign* emissions of CO_2.[19] Virtually any

---

18 Which is sometimes stated as 'the importance of being unimportant,' in the sense that the smaller (greater) the share of an input in cost the smaller (greater) will be the absolute value of the derived demand elasticity for the input. This law is valid in the present case, since the elasticity of product demand (around 1) clearly exceeds the elasticity of input substitution (we are referring to intermediate inputs which have an assumed elasticity of substitution of 0.25 in our model).

19 There is some controversy in international negotiation circles as to whether or not foreign-induced emissions should be 'counted' towards a country's contributions to changes in global carbon emissions. Apart from the obvious point of avoiding double-counting, this is a non-debate: of course they should. It is another matter to debate legal liability for policing foreign

domestic policy is going to have some impact on the structure of Swedish imports, as changes in the relative prices of domestic goods cause Swedes to substitute in favour for or against foreign goods. In the present case there will be substitution away from those goods whose input price, shown in percentage change form in Table 6.9 in column IPRICE%, has increased. The clearest instances are as expected, PETR and GASV. In each case there is a large increase in domestic prices brought about by the doubling of the carbon tax: after all of the general equilibrium effects have worked themselves out, the final domestic price increase is about 18 or 16 per cent. This results in a fall in domestic production, and a switch towards imports, shown in percentage change form in Table 6.9 in column IMP%. There is also a reduction in exports, shown in column EXP% in Table 6.9, for the same reason: Swedish exports in these carbon-intensive goods are simply unable to compete with foreign goods at (unchanged) world prices.

Hence we have an increase in the value of foreign imports of PETR and SMOR, and indeed in the physical quantity of imports. If we were to assume that foreign producers are just as carbon-efficient as Swedish producers in the same industry, then there would be an increase in carbon emissions overseas due to the increased foreign production needed to meet Sweden's increased import demand. In fact we assume that foreigners are *not* as carbon-efficient as Sweden, which is generally a plausible assumption apart from extremely nuclear-intensive countries. The exact assumptions as to how much 'dirtier' foreign production is[20] are not so important as the general logic that accounts for the foreign change in emissions. That logic is important since it is global emissions that matter for the final environmental good, reduced risk of *global* warming. Hence it is incumbent on Sweden to take into account the 'leakage' effects of just reducing onshore carbon-intensive activities and substituting offshore production of those products.

We acknowledge that we do not undertake a full multi-regional evaluation of this leakage issue, and there are obvious limitations to calculations of this kind. It is possible that changes in Sweden's exports will change production patterns overseas in ways that could increase or decrease carbon emissions globally. More generally, since we do not model the general equilibrium of foreign economies, we are not accounting for the full effects of changes in Sweden's net trade pattern. Given these qualifications, which are inherent to

---

economic activity induced by (internationally legal and acceptable) domestic policies (e.g., see Harrison (1994)). Our concern here is to inform the policy debate in Sweden, not to posture by generating strategically creative environmental accounts for negotiators.

20 Specifically, we assume that Japan is just as efficient (due to nuclear power use), as Norway (due to hydro power). The European Union countries are 50 per cent less efficient, the United States is 100 per cent less efficient, and the Rest of the World is 200 per cent less efficient. These aggregate efficiency measures are used to scaleup the sectoral emissions for Sweden, depending on the endogenous source of imports. It should be possible to refine these estimates of foreign emissions in time.

the use of a single economy model, we believe it important to acknowledge the *potentially* offsetting effects of carbon tax reforms when international trade is taken into account. There are, of course, many sectors where the foreign effect works in the same direction as the domestic effect (e.g., STEN), so our incorporation of foreign effects should not be viewed as imparting a presumptive bias into the estimation of global emissions.

The final column in Table 6.9, CO2_W, shows the aggregate world change in emissions of carbon in each sector. The foreign effects *tend* to be dominated by the domestic change, since imports are generally a much smaller percentage of domestic consumption in most sectors than domestic production.

C. Price and Production Impacts

The evaluation of welfare impacts and emissions impacts are, in an important sense, the 'bottom line' of our policy simulations since they provide the ultimate basis for evaluating the policy. By examining them one gets an idea of what is happening to the Swedish economy as the result of the C100 policy. However, it may be useful to look more directly at the changes in prices, production and trade to see the underlying causes of these effects.

From the IPRICE% column in Table 6.9 we see that the PETR and GASV sectors face a large price increase. Given the structure of carbon taxes, as shown in Table 6.3, these 'first order' impacts are not surprising.

Why do prices for PETR and GASV, however, only rise by about 17 per cent when the *ad valorem* rates of carbon taxes listed in Table 6.3 look to be anywhere from 15 up to 90 per cent? The answer is to recall that the higher rates do not apply to all sectors that use PETR and GASV, particularly energy-intensive manufacturing sectors. Thus if we average out the carbon tax rate on PETR and GASV over all sectors, including those that are exempt from it and are not listed in Table 6.3, the average rate would be closer to the observed price changes. In addition, the final price changes shown in Table 6.9 will reflect additional 'second-order' impacts due to resource re-allocations by consumers, producers and foreigners. Nonetheless, we would expect the first-order effects on prices to dominate for a scenario like this one.

Why is there such a small impact on the price of electricity, sector EL_O? Indeed, there is a slight increase in the price of sector EL_O, but it does not round up to 1 per cent and hence is shown as a 'blank' in our reports. Nonetheless, why is there not a larger increase, since EL_O *has* to be carbon-intensive? The immediate response is that Swedish electricity generation is dominated by nuclear and hydro, which are *not* carbon-intensive.

Essentially the same answer to this question comes from considering in detail the usage of intermediate inputs that are hit with the carbon tax, and then seeing what happens to their prices. Since we know that PETR and GASV have substantial price increases, the implication of a small price increase for EL_O is that it must not use very much of these as intermediate inputs. It is instructive in the economics of our model to work this issue through further.

Sector EL_O has five sources of primary energy inputs in our model.[21] Three are those listed in the columns of Table 6.3 as bearing carbon taxes: STEN, PETR and GASV. The fourth is SMOR, which does not bear any carbon taxes. The fifth is EL_O itself, which is where all of the nuclear-generated primary energy comes from in the Input-Output database. Of *these five* intermediate inputs, the cost shares in 1992 were: STEN 39 per cent, PETR 26 per cent, SMOR 0 per cent, GASV 15 per cent and EL_O 20 per cent. However, it would still seem that the taxes on STEN, PETR and GASV should impact EL_O prices. However, these percentages are misleading as to the complete cost structure of the EL_O sector. For example, the EL_O sector spent about as much on 'consulting and lobbying services' (Uppdragsverksamhet, or UPPD) in 1992 as it did on PETR, and while consultants and lobbyists obviously generate a lot of negative externalities they are not (yet) subject to any pollution tax!

As a share of *total* intermediate inputs, then, the cost shares in 1992 were much smaller: STEN 11 per cent, PETR 8 per cent and GASV 5 per cent. A simple piece of arithmetic suggests that the weighted carbon tax on EL_O from these three inputs is only 7.13 per cent = (0 per cent × 0.11) + (87 per cent × 0.08) + (61 per cent × 0.05). However, even this calculation overstates the effective tax in our model and the economy, since there are some possibilities for EL_O to substitute away from the more heavily taxed input PETR, and indeed away from all of the taxed inputs, since there are other inputs used in the benchmark technology to product it's output.[22]

D. Tax Replacement Schemes

The increase in carbon taxes in scenario C100 might be expected, *a priori*, to generate a net increase in government revenues in the absence of any other changes. Indeed this is in fact what happens in our model, at least before we

---

21 There is a sixth source: wood. There were substantial intermediate sales from the SKOG sector to the EL_O sector in 1992, comparable in value to sales from the GASV sector. These inputs represent the use of wood scraps to generate supplementary electricity in some specialized pulp factories. Since it is not liable for carbon taxes, we ignore it in our discussion.

22 The current specification of technology in our model does not differentiate energy inputs from non-energy inputs. Hence the derived elasticity of demand for UPPD would be about the same as for PETR in the model, given that the intermediate input cost shares are about the same for EL_O. An extension of the model could add this differentiation, allowing an extremely low elasticity of substitution between energy and non-energy inputs as composites, but some substitution between the items within each composite. In such a version it would be harder for EL_O to substitute away from taxed inputs. The only way it could do so would be to substitute towards the EL_O energy input, which we interpret as nuclear-generation. If we further added constraints on that avenue of 'escaping taxes by substitution,' such as specified in the N100 scenario, the EL_O sector would be hit *much* harder by the carbon tax increase.

allow relative prices to change to return the Swedish economy to a general equilibrium. When prices and behaviour changes, we discover that the carbon tax increase generates a net *increase* in government revenue as expected. The net increase requires a 1.5 per cent decrease in labour taxes to re-balance the government budget.

However, although net revenues increase due to the carbon tax increase, gross revenues from the energy tax actually decrease. How can such a 'perverse' effect on government revenues come about? In principle there is no surprise here, since it is possible that consumption and production may move away from products that already have a large tax. In practice, this is what happens. The large increase in revenues collected by the carbon tax is offset in part by a decrease in revenues collected under the energy tax. There are also decreases in taxes collected under the factor taxes and the VAT, but these are of 'second order' in comparison to the offset from the energy tax.[23]

Intuitively it is also easy to explain what is generating the qualitative result that the revenue effect from energy taxes offsets the revenue effect from carbon tax increases. The energy tax affects all manufacturing sectors without major exemptions, unlike the carbon tax. If the doubling of the carbon tax causes a decreased demand for products from those sectors, since they are now relatively less attractive than before due to the increase in their input costs brought about by the carbon tax, then there will be less demand for the products of sectors that bear the energy tax. Hence there may be some gains of revenue from the energy tax in those sectors which bear both the energy and carbon tax, but there will be offsetting losses in revenue from the energy tax in those sectors which bear only the energy tax. Depending on the elasticity of demand for those products, it is perfectly plausible that the net change in revenues from the energy tax will be negative: higher demand elasticities resulting in more revenue losses from the energy tax. Since the derived demand elasticity for energy-intensive intermediate inputs depends on both the direct elasticity of substitution between intermediates *and* the elasticity for the final products produced by sectors using energy relatively intensively, the formal simulations results discussed above are perfectly intuitive.

The 'bottom line' of these substitution effects on carbon tax revenues is easy to see in Table 6.11. The first series of columns show the tax revenues in billions of SEK from the carbon taxes in the benchmark, and the second series of columns show the change in tax revenues in scenario C100. For ease of interpretation and comparison we evaluate these changes in revenues using

---

23 In a formal sense it is easy to see what assumptions in the model generate this result. The first possibility is that there is a great deal of direct substitutability in terms of intermediate inputs *away* from the use of products that are 'hit' by the energy tax. This could occur because of the elasticity of substitution of 0.25 assumed between intermediate inputs. The second possibility is that there is an effect coming from the substitutability of *final* goods that use carbon and energy intensively.

benchmark prices. Just as with the interpretation of the tax *rates* listed in Table 6.3, the payments are from each row sector for their usage of the column input. The vast bulk of carbon tax revenues comes from inputs of PETR, and the lion's share of revenues in the PETR column of panels (a) and (b) comes from just a handful of sectors: SAMF, BYGG, VARU and EL_O.

We now consider the effect of using the VAT or lump-sum transfers to keep government expenditures constant after a 100 per cent increase in carbon taxes. The results are very similar to those found with the C100 scenario and labour tax replacement.

One implication of these small differences in the alternate use of labour taxes, the VAT and lump-sum taxes is that there seems to be relatively little distortionary impact from these replacement tax instruments. This may be an artifact of several model assumptions which could be examined further, such as the use of constant labour taxes for each household type, and for each household income level. A distinction between marginal and average labour tax rates would likely add significant distortions from the use of the labour tax.

On the other hand, the more important part of this 'tax replacement story' is not the size of the marginal excess burden (MEB) of the taxes but the fact that welfare *decreases* with the increase in carbon taxes irrespective of the tax replacement instrument. This outcome vitiates the 'double dividend' argument, which presumes that increases in carbon taxes will generate increased revenue that allow a reduction in highly distortionary taxes elsewhere in the economy. Even with the expected net increase in government revenues, we do not find a net welfare gain from any of the replacement schemes. Hence *the double dividend story does not hold here*, at least in the strong form that hypothesizes a possible net welfare gain.

On the other hand, there are some benefits from using the VAT or a lump-sum tax to replace revenues, relative to using labour taxes. The welfare cost of an average Kton of CO_2 reduced using the C100 scenario is 74 million SEK (= 3.9 billion SEK ÷ 52.2 Ktons of CO_2). But the welfare cost drops to an average of only 43 million SEK in scenario C100V and 39 million SEK in scenario C100LS. Since the lump-sum tax replacement option is not realistic in the sense of having a policy counterpart, we therefore tentatively recommend that the VAT be used as the tax replacement instrument instead of labour taxes. Again, this finding is conditional on our rudimentary treatment of income taxes in the model. Alternative specifications, discussed earlier, would increase the MEB of labour taxes to the point where they would be preferred to the VAT as a replacement instrument. Further work should be undertaken on this feature of the model before we could have more confidence in this particular finding.

6.3.3   Effects of Constraints on Nuclear Power

Although the model does not distinguish 'nuclear' components of the
electricity generation industry EL_O, it is possible to examine the effects of
carbon tax changes with a rudimentary representation of the political
constraint on nuclear power in Sweden. We do so by recognizing that nuclear
power is roughly 50 per cent of the current domestic power supplied in
Sweden, and that it has a very low carbon-intensity under normal operating
circumstances. Constraints on the production of EL_O can be imposed on our
model, providing some economic instrument is also added to ensure that the
constraint is met. The most natural is simply a tax on domestic value added in
the EL_O sector, set such that the industry does not find it 'economical' to
produce at any higher level.

We impose constraints in this fashion that correspond to the EL_O
industry not being allowed to expand relative to the benchmark (N100), and
to it having to contract to 75 per cent of the benchmark. This 75 per cent
contraction may be viewed as half-way towards the goal of complete
elimination of nuclear. In each case we also impose the scenario C100, so
these constraints should be evaluated relative to the impacts for C100
discussed earlier.

The nature of these constraints on EL_O also suggest that we should
carefully interpret the carbon emissions estimates. If we were just allowing
EL_O to change, without regard to whether it is the 'cleanest of the clean'
electricity plant or the 'dirtiest of the dirty,' then we would just apply the
industry-wide carbon emissions coefficient for that sector. This is exactly
what we do in all other simulations, since our model is otherwise silent on the
composition of the EL_O activity.[24] But here we are explicitly trying to
capture the effects of nuclear reductions, so it is appropriate for us to modify
our carbon emissions for sector EL_O accordingly. We therefore set all
carbon emissions for this sector equal to their benchmark level, implicitly
assuming that nuclear-generated electricity generates no carbon emissions at
all. As a first approximation to the dirtier alternatives, this is acceptable.

The detailed sectoral results for scenario N75 are shown in Table 6.12, and
the aggregate impacts of the scenarios with nuclear constraints are reported in
Table 6.10. In welfare terms there is a substantial increase in the 'price tag' of
the carbon tax increase (from 3.9 billion SEK to 7.8 billion SEK) as we move
from scenario N100 to N75, and a sharp increase in the aggregate reduction
in domestic carbon emissions (from 47 Ktons to 229 Ktons). There are
modest changes in foreign emissions, such that the global reduction in

---

24 Actually, since the model solves for the intermediate inputs used by EL_O, and one might be
able to identify those as being associated with 'dirty' or 'clean' technologies, it would be
possible to allow carbon emissions to capture these effects. We prefer to model such detail
when we have more information on the technology of each activity used in the EL_O industry.

emissions is driven again by the change in domestic emissions.[25] The main reason for the increase in carbon emission reductions is generally the depressing effect of the nuclear power constraint on domestic production. Despite the larger welfare cost of reducing carbon emissions with the nuclear constraint the reduction in carbon emission is even larger, such that the price tag of carbon reductions is lower with this constraint in place. Specifically, the welfare cost of an average Kton of CO_2 reduced in scenario N100 is only 34 million SEK (= 7.8 billion SEK ÷ 229 Ktons), compared to 74 million SEK in scenario C100 and 43 million SEK in scenario C100V.

Despite the possibility that they could interact, it appears that the carbon tax reductions and the nuclear constraint are roughly 'additive' in effects. Scenario NU75 imposes a 75 per cent constraint on sector EL_O, but without the doubling of the carbon tax. It therefore looks at the 'pure' effect of the nuclear constraint. The aggregate results, also shown in Table 6.10, are virtually the same as the simple difference between the results for C100 and N75.

These aggregate results do mask a substantial restructuring of Swedish industry, however, as seen in Table 6.12. With a 25 per cent reduction in domestic value added, and a substantial tax on value added, electricity prices rise by 55 per cent and generate large changes in relative prices in most other sectors. The biggest losers in terms of domestic production are those that are relatively intensive users of electricity, of course: JARN, A_ME, PAPP, PPPP, CEME, JRN_, FERR, META and GASV. In many of these industries domestic production is partially replaced by imports, but in most cases there is a substantial reduction in demand for the product (whether produced by domestic or foreign producers). With such widespread devastation of some major Swedish industries, it is no surprise that one sector to *expand* is our old friend, the 'consulting and lobbying' sector (UPPD)! Indeed, there are many sectors that expand slightly as the result of the nuclear shutdown: LAKE, GUMM, machinery industries (e.g., MSKN, ELMO and INST), transportation (e.g., BILA and FLYG), and some service sectors (e.g., EGNA and OVRP).

6.3.4   A Cost-Benefit Comparison

Our model is constructed to generate estimates for each household of the 'price tag' or cost of increases in carbon taxes. Is it possible to relate these, even roughly, to estimates of gross benefits from carbon tax reductions?

---

25 The largest increase in emissions, not surprisingly, is for imports of sector EL_O. It is an open issue if these would indeed be carbon-intensive. If generated from Norwegian hydro-electric sources they probably would not, but if generated by German coal they may be. Our model is currently silent on these possibilities, although it should be possible to refine the estimate of foreign carbon emissions to capture these differential effects.

Although proper gross benefit estimates do not exist for Sweden, or indeed for any country, there have been some estimates floated in international circles that can be usefully related to our cost estimates.

The source for these gross benefit estimates is the Inter-Governmental Panel on Climate Change (IPCC), specifically Working Group 3.[26] Based on some loose 'avoided cost' calculations, they tentatively offer USD 125 per *ton of carbon* as an upper increase in gross benefits. We carefully translate that into *Ktons of CO_2* for comparison with our model, and then into SEK from USD.

The IPCC report does not indicate if they intend this number to refer to individuals or households, so we apply it to both. The IPCC report also does not say if this estimate is an *aggregate* over individuals or households, or is meant to be interpreted *per* individual or *per* household. Since the underlying avoided cost calculations are aggregative in nature, we assume that this estimate applies as an aggregate. To be conservative, we further assume that it applies to the aggregate population (of individuals or households) in *Sweden*, and not the *planet*. We then apportion the benefits proportionally across households, according to that household's share of the aggregate number of individuals or households. This assumption is appropriate given that we have no priors or data to suggest that one household group would value carbon reductions any greater than another.

We further assume that this gross benefit estimate is linear in the Kton reduction in CO_2 that our model generates for any particular scenario. In the case of C100, we estimate a 52.2 Kton reduction, so we are in effect assuming that each household receives the same gross benefit from the first Kton reduction as from the last. Although we might justify such an assumption based on the small scale of this carbon reduction, and hence the approximate linearity of the unknown marginal benefit schedule, our primary concern is to keep the arithmetic simple and transparent. It should *not* be assumed that marginal benefit would decline, due to diminishing marginal utility arguments, since households may correctly perceive the importance of threshold effects in carbon reductions. In other words, I might not be willing to pay anything for small decreases in carbon emissions, but substantially more if I perceive that the aggregate emission reduction might make a difference to the risk of global warming.

Our cost estimates do, however, take into account the non-linearity of the underlying preferences and technologies for larger and larger reductions in emissions.

The resulting estimates for each household are presented in Table 6.13. The last row shows the average benefit and cost over all households, and each row shows the arithmetic for each household. We use an estimate of the gross

---

26 The source for these estimates is their summary report, available on web site http://www.unep.ch/ipcc/sumwg3.html. The estimates appear near the end of §7 of that report.

benefit which is actually double the upper bound of the IPCC estimate, so as to avoid any risk of understating those benefits.

The conclusion is clear. The benefits of increasing the carbon tax in Sweden are a tiny fraction of the 'price tag' which Swedes must pay in the form of higher prices and reduced incomes. Although we do not put much credence in these gross benefit numbers, they do serve to highlight the basis of our conclusion that carbon tax increases are not currently justifiable in Sweden. They also serve to focus the debate on the net benefits of further carbon taxes onto the question of estimating gross benefits for Swedes. *If these numbers are correct*, then advocates of carbon tax increases are telling the average Swede that he or she must pay a lot more for some environmental good than that Swede appears to derive as a benefit. This might be because the *advocate* derives significant enough benefits and would be willing to pay the price tag, but that does not justify forcing the price on others.

6.4 CONCLUSIONS

Our most important conclusion is that the effects of the existing carbon tax in Sweden are surprisingly counter-intuitive. The *a priori* beliefs which we started with reflected that intuition and the prevailing 'conventional wisdom': that the exemptions for manufacturing would probably diminish the impact on carbon emissions, but that otherwise the tax was well targeted at the externality in question and ought to have a dramatic effect. If combined with a reduction in taxes on some highly distortionary tax, such as the labour tax, it could provide an attractive means of meeting the environmental goal at minimum cost. Maybe a double dividend was too much to hope for, but some benefit from the tax replacement could be expected.

The results presented here, if correct, undermine this conclusion in several respects.

First, increases in the carbon tax itself has relatively 'modest' impact on aggregate carbon emissions. The reason is that there are many avenues of substitution open in terms of production and consumption choices, such that attempts to tax certain externalities in some sectors generate an incentive to expand other sectors. The only interesting question is whether the net impact on carbon emissions will be positive: there should be no sensible debate on the fact that some sectors will emit more carbon when the carbon tax is increased while some reduce carbon emissions.

Second, increasing carbon taxes results in a net increase in government tax revenues, just as a partial equilibrium analysis would predict. However, it induces offsetting increases and decreases from different tax bases, such that it is conceivable that there could be a net decrease under certain circumstances (e.g., extremely high trade elasticities). The reason is that the carbon tax induces significant substitution in inputs and between products, resulting in a reduction in the use of inputs or products that would otherwise be paying substantial energy taxes. Normally these effects would be of 'second order,' such that an increase in one tax would be expected to increase revenue. However, the close overlap of the energy and carbon taxes in terms of legal incidence, combined with the greater magnitude of the energy taxes in the base year in *ad valorem* and revenue terms for some sectors, means that these second order effects cannot be completely neglected in this case. Nonetheless, the net revenue effects on carbon tax revenues is much larger than the net revenue effects on energy tax revenues.

Third, imposed constraints on the nuclear generation of electricity would significantly enhance the reductions in carbon emissions flowing from carbon tax increases. This effect comes from a general decline in energy-intensive production in Sweden, due to energy price increases. Despite an increase in the *aggregate* welfare cost, nuclear constraints lower the *average* welfare cost of carbon reductions.

Finally, our 'bottom line' is that simple *expansions* in the existing carbon tax carry too high a price tag for most Swedish households to be justifiable. This overall cost-benefit assessment rests on some admittedly fragile estimates of the gross benefit that Swedes will get from carbon reductions. Our job was only to generate the gross costs of those policies, and for that side of the 'cost-benefit equation' our model is relatively well suited. However, if the gross benefit estimates currently in use in international carbon tax debates are to be believed, Sweden cannot justify further *unilateral* increases in carbon taxes.

These results may not be what everyone likes to hear. Since we are not naïve to the political pressures surrounding this issue in Sweden, nor so cynical as to dismiss them as being unworthy of debate, it is incumbent on us to attempt to direct debate on our model and its results into productive areas.

The model is incomplete in terms of a number of important *parameters*. Specifically, we need to (1) add better data on the differences in factor endowments of households, to better reflect differences in their income sources; (2) incorporate data-based estimates of leisure consumption in the benchmark, as well as labour supply elasticities for different household types; and (3) employ data-based estimates of differences in carbon emissions in foreign countries relative to Sweden. As revised estimates for these parameters are generated they can be introduced directly into the existing model immediately.

The model may also be incomplete in terms of its treatment of the *economic structure* of some sectors. Specifically, we could (1) provide a richer specification of the production technology of sectors with respect to energy inputs (e.g., allowing energy to be an input that combines with other intermediates in a Leontief manner, but which incorporates some degree of substitutability between energy types; and the use of non-separable production functions); (2) incorporate some supply restrictions on imports in key sectors, particularly those such as electricity which may be constrained by resource availability and/or network logistics; (3) model the way in which labour taxes impact households in a way that captures differences between marginal and average rates, as well as differences across households; (4) model the effects of labour unemployment, including implications for unemployment benefits and the government budget; and (5) model the use of nuclear and non-nuclear technologies more explicitly, perhaps with a formal sub-model of the electricity sector. Each of these extensions are conceptually straightforward, and use relatively familiar modelling tools, but are beyond the scope of the current project. We believe that each could be significant for current policy purposes.

The model could also be evaluated in terms of more *radical changes in structure*. Specifically, we could consider (1) incorporating measures of environmental benefits[27] explicitly into the household utility function, to allow a complete cost-benefit analysis to be undertaken; (2) explicit dynamics, with attention given to the rate at which households and firms discount future environmental benefits relative to current costs; (3) lobbying activities surrounding green tax reforms, and endogenous political activity over the selection of reforms; and (4) endogenous technical change induced by carbon taxes. Each of these entail exciting methodological extensions.

---

27 Some analysts have proposed using the estimated cost of the *existing* carbon tax structure as a crude measure of the environmental benefits from reduced emissions. We regard this inference as problematic, to put it politely. At *best* it could be inferred that the murky political process leading to the existing tax level represents the median voter, and then only if one were to make heroic assumptions about that political process representing the outcome 'as if' a series of dichotomous-choice referenda had been undertaken at alternative tax-prices. Although a matter of some controversy (e.g., see Harrison and Kriström (1995)), such inferences cannot even be made if one uses a hypothetical survey to mimic the results of real referenda of this type (see Cummings, Elliot, Harrison and Murphy (1996)). Even assuming away these problems, knowing the marginal value that the *median* voter places on some public good tells us nothing whatsoever about the distribution of benefits, at least in the absence of super-heroic assumptions that would make even *Fantomen* blush. Without information on that distribution one cannot say anything about the net impact on welfare of individual households, or even about the aggregate impact under simplifying utilitarian assumptions. There is simply no acceptable substitute for estimating those benefits directly, and accounting fully for the potential biases in hypothetical survey elicitation procedures (e.g., see Blackburn, Harrison and Rutström (1994)).

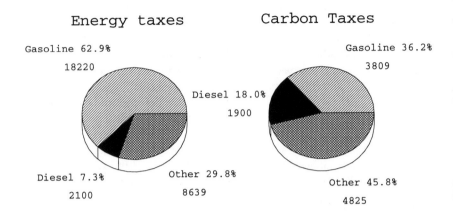

Figure 6.1 Revenues from energy taxes in 1994 (millions of SEK)

Table 6.1   *Sectors in the Swedish model*

JORD	JORDBRUK	Agriculture and Hunting
SKOG	SKOGSBRUK	Forestry and Logging
FSKE	FISKE	Fishing
JARN	JARNGRUVOR	Iron Ore Mining
A_ME	A MET.GRUVOR	Other Metal Mining
STEN	STENBROTT A.GR.	Stone Quarrying and Other Non-Metallic Mining
SLAK	SLAKTERIER	Meat Slaughtering
MEJE	MEJERIER	Dairy Products
FRUK	FRUKTKONSERVER	Canning of Fruits and Vegetables
FISK	FISKKONSERVER	Canning of Fish
FETT	FETT OLJOR	Oils and Fats
KVAR	KVARNPRODUKTER	Grain Mill Production
BAGE	BAGERIPROD.	Bakery Products
SOCK	SOCKER	Sugar
CHOK	CHOKLAD KONF.	Confectionary
DIVX	DIV.LIVSMEDEL	Other Food
FODE	FODERMEDEL	Prepared Animal Feeds
DRYC	DRYCKER	Beverages
TOBA	TOBAK	Tobacco
GARN	GARN VAVNAD	Spinning and Weaving
TEXT	TEXTILSOMN.	Textiles Other than Clothing
TRIK	TRIK2VAROR	Hosiery and Knitted Goods
OVRT	OVR TEXTIL	Other Textiles
BEKL	BEKLADNAD	Clothing
LADE	LADER SKOR	Leather and Shoes
S2GV	S2GVERK	Wood Preparations
TRAH	TRAHUS SNICK.	Wooden Building Materials
A_TR	A TRAMATERIAL	Other Wooden Materials
OVR_	OVR TRAVAROR	Other Wood Products
TRAM	TRAMOBLER	Wooden Furniture
PAPP	PAPPERSMASSA	Paper Pulp
PPPP	PAPPER PAPP	Paper and Board Manufacturing
TRAF	TRAFIBERPL.	Fibreboard
PFRP	PAPPFORP.	Paper Packaging Products
OVRX	OVR. PAPPER	Other Paper Products
GRAF	GRAFISK IND	Printing and Publishing
KEMI	KEMIKALIER	General Chemicals
GODS	GODSELMEDEL	Fertilizers and Pesticides
BASP	BASPLAST	Plastics and Synthetic Fibres
PLAS	PLAST HALVF.	Semi-finished Plastic Products
FARG	FARG	Paints
LAKE	LAKEMEDEL	Drugs and Medicines
TVAT	TVATTMEDEL	Soaps and Detergents
OVRK	OVR KEMIK.	Other Chemical Products
PETR	PETROL.RAFF	Petroleum Refining
SMOR	SMORJMEDEL	Lubricating Oils and Greases
GUMM	GUMMIVAROR	Rubber Products

PLSV	PLASTVAROR	Plastic Products
PORS	PORSLIN	Pottery
GLAS	GLAS	Glass and Glass Products
TEGE	TEGEL	Structural Clay Products
CEME	CEMENT	Cement and Plaster
OVRM	OVR MINERAL	Other Non-Metallic Mineral Products
JRN_	JRN O ST2L	Iron and Steel
FERR	FERROLEGERING	Ferro-Alloys Manufacturing
JNGJ	JNGJUTERIER	Iron and Steel Casting
META	METALLVERK	Metal Fabrication
METV	METALLVALSV.	Metal Rolling Mills
I_JA	I JARNGJUTERI	Iron and Steel Casting
METR	METALLVAROR	Other Metal Casting
MSKN	MASKINER	Industrial Machinery
ELMO	ELMOTORER	Electrical Machinery
TELE	TELEPRODUKTER	Electronics and Telecommunications
HUSH	HUSH2LLSMASK.	Domestic Electrical Appliances
OVRE	OVR.ELPROD.	Other Electrical Goods
VARV	VARV B2TAR	Ship Building and Repair
RALS	RALSFORDON	Railway Building and Repair
BILA	BILAR	Motor Vehicles and Parts
CYKL	CYKLAR	Bicycles and Motorcycles
FLYG	FLYGPLAN	Aircraft Manufacture and Repair
OVRR	OVR TRANSP.M.	Other Transport Equipment
INST	INSTRUMENT	Scientific Instruments
A_TI	A TILLVERKN.	Other Manufacturing
EL_O	EL O VARMEVERK	Electricity and Steam
GASV	GASVERK	Gas
VATT	VATTENVERK	Water
BYGG	BYGGNAD	Construction
VARU	VARUHANDEL	Trade
HOTE	HOTELL REST.	Hotels and Restaurants
SAMF	SAMFARDSEL	Transport and Storage
POST	POST TELE	Communication
BANK	BANK FORSAKR.	Banks and Insurance
EGNA	EGNAHEM FRITID	Housing
FAST	FASTIGHETSFORV.	Other Real Estate
UPPD	UPPDRAGSV.	Business Services
REPA	REPARATIONER	Repair Services
OVRP	OVR. PR. TJ	Personal Services

Table 6.2   Households in the Swedish model

S_NC_1	Single adults with no children - first quartile
S_NC_2	Single adults with no children - second quartile
S_NC_3	Single adults with no children - third quartile
S_NC_4	Single adults with no children - fourth quartile
S_C_1	Single adults with children - bottom half
S_C_2	Single adults with children - top half
M_NC_1	Multiple adults with no children - first quartile
M_NC_2	Multiple adults with no children - second quartile
M_NC_3	Multiple adults with no children - third quartile
M_NC_4	Multiple adults with no children - fourth quartile
M_1C_1	Multiple adults with 1 child - first quartile
M_1C_2	Multiple adults with 1 child - second quartile
M_1C_3	Multiple adults with 1 child - third quartile
M_1C_4	Multiple adults with 1 child - fourth quartile
M_2C_1	Multiple adults with 2 children - first quartile
M_2C_2	Multiple adults with 2 children - second quartile
M_2C_3	Multiple adults with 2 children - third quartile
M_2C_4	Multiple adults with 2 children - fourth quartile
M_3C_1	Multiple adults with 3 or more children - first quartile
M_3C_2	Multiple adults with 3 or more children - second quartile
M_3C_3	Multiple adults with 3 or more children - third quartile
M_3C_4	Multiple adults with 3 or more children - fourth quartile
O_NC_1	Others with no children - first quartile
O_NC_2	Others with no children - second quartile
O_NC_3	Others with no children - third quartile
O_NC_4	Others with no children - fourth quartile
O_C_1	Others with children - first quartile
O_C_2	Others with children - second quartile
O_C_3	Others with children - third quartile
O_C_4	Others with children - fourth quartile

Table 6.3   Benchmark carbon taxes (per cent)

		Input	
Purchasing Sector	STEN	PETR	GASV
JORD	268	64	61
SKOG		59	61
FSKE		66	61
JARN	268	84	61
A_ME	268	90	61
STEN		67	61
SLAK	67	19	15
MEJE	67	20	15
FRUK	67	21	15
FISK	67	19	15
FETT	67	20	15
KVAR	67	18	15
BAGE	67	18	15
SOCK	67	24	15
CHOK	67	22	15
DIVX	67	20	15
FODE	67	21	15
DRYC	67	20	15
TOBA	67	20	15
GARN		22	15
TEXT		17	15
TRIK		18	15
OVRT		19	15
BEKL		15	15
LADE		15	15
S2GV	67	18	15
TRAH	67	18	15
A_TR	67	23	15
OVR_	67	16	15
TRAM	67	17	15
PAPP	67	24	15
PPPP		24	15
TRAF	67	25	15
PFRP	67	21	15
OVRX	67	19	15
GRAF	67	13	15
KEMI	67	20	15
GODS	67	19	15
BASP	67	23	15
PLAS	67	21	15
FARG	67	15	15
LAKE	67	22	15
TVAT	67	15	15
OVRK	67	20	15

Table 6.3   (continued)

PETR		25	15
SMOR	67	21	15
GUMM	67	18	15
PLSV	67	17	15
PORS		18	15
GLAS		20	15
TEGE		19	15
CEME		20	15
OVRM		19	15
JRN_	67	20	15
FERR	67	20	15
JNGJ	67	21	15
META	67	20	15
METV	67	20	15
I_JA	67	20	15
METR	67	17	15
MSKN	67	16	15
ELMO	67	14	15
TELE	67	17	15
HUSH	67	17	15
OVRE	67	16	15
VARV	67	18	15
RALS	67	18	15
BILA	67	16	15
CYKL	67	18	15
FLYG	67	14	15
OVRR	67	18	15
INST	67	12	15
A_TI		16	15
EL_O		87	61
GASV	268	87	61
VATT			61
BYGG		58	61
VARU		55	61
HOTE		55	61
SAMF		66	61
POST		55	61
BANK		55	61
EGNA		76	61
FAST		76	61
UPPD		55	61
REPA		55	61
OVRP	268	55	61

Table 6.4   Benchmark energy and sulphur taxes (per cent)

(a) Energy Taxes

	Input		
Purchasing Sector	STEN	PETR	GASV
JORD	77	108	16
SKOG		117	16
FSKE		111	16
JARN	77		16
A_ME	77		16
STEN	77		16
EL_O	77	68	16
GASV	77	68	16
VATT			16
BYGG		112	16
VARU		110	16
HOTE		110	16
SAMF		109	16
POST		110	16
BANK		110	16
EGNA		70	16
FAST		70	16
UPPD		110	16
REPA		110	16
OVRP	77	110	16

(b) Sulphur Taxes

	Input	
Purchasing Sector	STEN	PETR
JORD	56	0.5
SKOG		0.2
JARN	56	5
A_ME	56	7
STEN	56	0.3
EL_O		7
GASV	56	7
BYGG		0.1
SAMF		3
EGNA		2
FAST		2
OVRP		56

Table 6.5   Simulation scenarios

BENCH	Maintain all policies at their initial level and replicate the benchmark economy.
C100	**Increase the existing structure of carbon taxes in Sweden by 100 per cent above their benchmark rates, maintaining the existing exemptions from carbon taxes. Reduce labour taxes to maintain constant government revenue.**
C100V	Same as C100, except uses proportional adjustments in the VAT to ensure that government revenue is unchanged from the benchmark. These VAT adjustments are proportionally the same across all sectors to which the VAT is applied.
C100LS	Same as C100, except uses a lump-sum tax to ensure that government revenue is unchanged from the benchmark. Each household pays the lump-sum tax in proportion to their benchmark income.
N100	Same as C100, except that the activity level of the Electricity sector must be maintained at no more than 100 per cent of its benchmark level to reflect the constraint of no *expansion* of nuclear power.
N75	Same as N100, except that Electricity only be allowed to produce 75 per cent of its benchmark output.
NU75	Constrain Electricity to produce no more than 75 per cent of its benchmark output.

Table 6.6 Labour types in the Swedish model (per cent employment in sector)

| | Blue Collar | | | White Collar | | | | | |
Sector	L_BC_U	L_BC_S	L_BC	L_WC_U	L_WC_SS	L_WC_S	L_WC	L_EMP	L_SE
JORD	18	11	29	6	4	6	16	46	54
SKOG	40	15	55	10	12	11	33	89	11
FSKE	25	3	28	4	5	56	65	92	8
JARN	35	30	65	6	17	8	31	97	3
A_ME	35	34	69	7	13	7	27	96	4
STEN	26	15	40	16	18	19	52	93	7
SLAK	41	25	66	11	8	9	28	94	6
MEJE	47	7	54	18	12	12	41	95	5
FRUK	41	7	48	17	13	17	47	95	5
FISK	56	4	60	11	8	13	33	93	7
FETT	32	13	45	13	18	19	50	95	5
KVAR	31	15	46	12	13	22	47	93	7
BAGE	40	23	63	14	6	10	30	93	7
SOCK	32	25	57	9	14	13	37	94	6
CHOK	48	8	56	15	11	13	39	94	6
DIVX	39	8	47	18	12	16	47	94	6
FODE	38	11	50	20	9	16	45	95	5
DRYC	43	8	52	15	13	14	41	93	7
TOBA	45	14	59	8	13	15	37	96	4
GARN	55	7	63	12	10	10	32	95	5
TEXT	55	8	64	12	6	12	31	94	6
TRIK	61	7	67	11	8	9	29	96	4
OVRT	42	10	51	11	12	20	43	95	5
BEKL	57	10	67	10	7	11	27	94	6
LADE	58	8	66	9	5	14	28	95	5
S2GV	60	13	73	8	6	8	22	96	4
TRAH	30	34	64	10	11	11	32	96	4
A_TR	56	16	72	8	9	8	24	96	4
OVR_	57	11	68	8	9	9	26	94	6
TRAM	42	27	69	8	8	11	26	95	5
PAPP	34	31	65	10	15	8	32	97	3
PPPP	40	21	62	11	14	10	35	97	3
TRAF	45	22	67	9	11	10	29	96	4
PFRP	37	17	55	13	14	14	41	96	4
OVRX	38	20	58	13	10	16	38	96	4
GRAF	14	29	43	17	22	12	50	93	7
KEMI	18	20	38	13	23	21	57	95	5
GODS	26	27	53	9	15	17	41	95	5
BASP	24	25	49	13	21	13	47	96	4
PLAS	43	13	56	11	12	16	40	95	5
FARG	31	6	37	19	19	20	58	94	6
LAKE	15	6	20	13	27	35	75	96	4
TVAT	33	4	37	25	13	20	57	94	6
OVRK	35	14	49	13	17	17	47	96	4
PETR	13	23	35	10	35	14	60	95	5
SMOR	31	10	40	17	20	18	54	94	6
GUMM	54	6	61	9	12	12	34	95	5
PLSV	49	12	61	10	11	12	33	94	6

Table 6.6   (continued)

PORS	48	13	61	10	12	13	35	96	4
GLAS	51	17	68	8	10	10	28	96	4
TEGE	42	14	56	15	12	13	40	96	4
CEME	32	22	54	12	14	16	42	96	4
OVRM	44	15	59	11	14	11	36	96	4
JRN_	40	23	63	9	15	10	34	97	3
FERR	43	24	67	10	9	9	28	95	5
JNGJ	45	24	68	7	11	8	26	94	6
META	42	24	67	9	12	8	29	96	4
METV	43	17	60	11	14	11	36	96	4
I_JA	47	23	70	6	11	8	25	95	5
METR	31	31	62	8	12	12	32	95	5
MSKN	16	31	48	10	21	17	48	95	5
ELMO	17	27	44	9	25	18	52	95	5
TELE	15	16	31	10	31	23	63	95	5
HUSH	33	28	60	9	14	11	34	94	6
OVRE	27	23	49	10	21	15	46	95	5
VARV	15	41	56	7	17	14	38	94	6
RALS	17	48	65	6	16	9	31	96	4
BILA	34	22	57	6	20	12	38	95	5
CYKL	44	13	57	13	12	14	39	96	4
FLYG	12	28	39	8	31	18	57	97	3
OVRR	41	20	61	10	11	15	35	96	4
INST	12	21	33	11	26	24	62	95	5
A_TI	33	23	56	13	9	16	38	94	6
EL_O	7	28	35	11	36	14	61	97	3
GASV	4	15	19	11	28	35	74	93	7
VATT	6	46	53	9	27	8	44	97	3
BYGG	19	11	30	10	29	21	60	90	10
VARU	26	8	35	26	11	21	59	94	6
HOTE	25	27	52	12	13	10	35	88	12
SAMF	40	9	49	17	11	15	44	93	7
POST	54	2	56	17	13	10	40	96	4
BANK	2	1	2	27	37	30	93	95	5
EGNA	26	15	41	19	19	15	53	94	6
FAST	5	3	8	19	26	38	83	91	9
UPPD	6	46	53	13	7	21	41	94	6
REPA	23	20	43	15	5	30	49	93	7
OVRP	26	15	40	16	18	19	52	93	7
TOTAL	26	15	41	16	18	19	54	95	8

Table 6.7   Carbon emissions in the Swedish model

Sectors	Aggregate Emissions (1000 tons)	Per cent of Domestic Emissions	Rank of Per cent of Emissions	Cumulative Per cent	Emissions per billion SEK output	Rank of Per Unit Emissions
JORD	1388	3	10	77	29	21
SKOG	424	1	21	88	16	25
FSKE	192		34	95	96	11
JARN	266	1	27	92	73	13
A_ME	214		29	93	70	14
STEN	70		47	97	3	62
SLAK	113		38	96	3	64
MEJE	118		36	95	5	48
FRUK	57		52	98	5	47
FISK	39		61	99	5	44
FETT	38		62	99	6	40
KVAR	35		65	99	7	35
BAGE	98		41	96	6	42
SOCK	116		37	96	48	17
CHOK	57		53	98	6	39
DIVX	60		48	98	6	41
FODE	47		56	98	7	36
DRYC	98		42	97	3	59
TOBA	33		67	99	2	69
GARN	59		51	98	8	32
TEXT	17		80	100	3	66
TRIK	18		78	100	1	81
OVRT	19		77	100	3	65
BEKL	7		84	100		86
LADE	3		86	100		85
S2GV	98		40	96	4	51
TRAH	45		58	99	5	49
A_TR	27		70	100	6	38
OVR_	6		85	100	2	77
TRAM	28		69	99	1	79
PAPP	434	1	20	87	32	20
PPPP	398	1	22	89	9	30
TRAF	368	1	23	90	646	4
PFRP	95		43	97	15	26
OVRX	79		45	97	6	43
GRAF	105		39	96	2	70
KEMI	74		46	97	3	55
GODS	16		81	100	5	46
BASP	39		60	99	3	63
PLAS	53		54	98	5	45
FARG	21		73	100	3	57
LAKE	60		49	98	3	58
TVAT	17		79	100	2	71
OVRK	48		55	98	3	56
PETR	81		44	97	1	80
SMOR	59		50	98	16	24
GUMM	23		72	100	2	72
PLSV	46		57	99	3	61

Table 6.7   (continued)

PORS	179		35	95	65	15
GLAS	326	1	24	90	41	19
TEGE	213		30	93	147	8
CEME	225		28	92	166	7
OVRM	326	1	25	91	24	22
JRN_	2404	5	3	49	64	16
FERR	2404	5	3	49	1565	1
JNGJ	2348	5	5	58	1220	3
META	2170	4	6	63	264	5
METV	2160	4	7	67	217	6
I_JA	2155	4	8	71	1289	2
METR	208		33	94	3	68
MSKN	211		31	94	2	76
ELMO	20		74	100	2	75
TELE	33		68	99	1	83
HUSH	12		82	100	2	73
OVRE	37		63	99	1	78
VARV	37		64	99	5	50
RALS	33		66	99	8	31
BILA	209		32	94	2	74
CYKL	19		76	100	7	34
FLYG	44		59	99	3	67
OVRR	20		75	100	22	23
INST	24		71	100	1	82
A_TI	8		83	100	1	84
EL_O	9622	19	2	44	136	9
GASV	266	1	26	91	134	10
VATT			87	100		87
BYGG	1474	3	9	74	8	33
VARU	538	1	12	79	47	18
HOTE	538	1	12	79	12	28
SAMF	12352	25	1	25	80	12
POST	538	1	12	79	12	29
BANK	538	1	12	79	7	37
EGNA	459	1	18	85	4	54
FAST	459	1	18	85	4	52
UPPD	538	1	12	79	3	60
REPA	538	1	12	79	14	27
OVRP	538	1	11	78	4	53
TOTAL	50029	100				

Table 6.8   Welfare impact of doubling the carbon tax (scenario C100)

| | Per cent Share of... | | | EV in SEK per... | |
| | | | Utility | | |
Household	Households	Individuals	Index	Individual	Household
S_NC_2	9.1	4.2	99.8	-283.0	-283.0
S_NC_3	9.1	4.2	99.8	-409.0	-409.0
S_NC_4	9.2	4.2	99.9	-345.0	-345.0
S_C_1	1.8	1.9	99.8	-226.0	-521.0
S_C_2	1.8	2.2	99.7	-431.0	-1164.0
M_NC_1	7.3	6.7	99.5	-617.0	-1234.0
M_NC_2	7.4	6.8	99.7	-464.0	-928.0
M_NC_3	7.3	6.7	99.6	-653.0	-1307.0
M_NC_4	7.3	6.7	99.7	-693.0	-1387.0
M_1C_1	1.9	2.6	99.6	-386.0	-1157.0
M_1C_2	1.9	2.5	99.6	-448.0	-1343.0
M_1C_3	1.9	2.6	99.6	-537.0	-1611.0
M_1C_4	1.9	2.6	99.6	-762.0	-2287.0
M_2C_1	2.4	4.4	99.5	-416.0	-1666.0
M_2C_2	2.4	4.4	99.5	-481.0	-1924.0
M_2C_3	2.4	4.4	99.4	-602.0	-2407.0
M_2C_4	2.4	4.4	99.4	-758.0	-3033.0
M_3C_1	1.1	2.5	99.6	-299.0	-1557.0
M_3C_2	1.1	2.5	99.6	-363.0	-1887.0
M_3C_3	1.1	2.5	99.5	-461.0	-2397.0
M_3C_4	1.1	2.6	99.5	-537.0	-2900.0
O_NC_1	1.4	1.4	99.7	-436.0	-959.0
O_NC_2	1.4	1.7	99.7	-418.0	-1128.0
O_NC_3	1.4	1.8	99.7	-542.0	-1571.0
O_NC_4	1.4	2.1	99.7	-562.0	-1911.0
O_C_1	0.9	1.6	99.7	-348.0	-1323.0
O_C_2	0.9	1.8	99.7	-320.0	-1375.0
O_C_3	0.9	1.8	99.7	-456.0	-1963.0
O_C_4	0.9	1.9	99.6	-569.0	-2562.0

Table 6.9   Sectoral impact of doubling the carbon tax (scenario C100)

Sector	IPRICE%	VA%	IMP%	EXP%	CO2_D	CO2_F	CO2_W
JORD				-1	-1	1	
SKOG	-1		-1				-1
FSKE				-1	-1		-1
JARN		-1		-2	-4		-4
A_ME				-1			
STEN		-6	-7	-7	-5	-8	-13
SLAK	-1						
MEJE				-1			
FRUK	-1						
FISK	-1						
FETT	-1						
KVAR	-1						
BAGE	-1						
SOCK	1			-1			
CHOK	-1						
DIVX	-1						
DRYC	-1						
TOBA	-1	1					
GARN	-1						
TEXT	-1	1	-1				
TRIK	-1	1		1			
OVRT	-1	1					
BEKL	-1	1					
LADE	-1	1					
S2GV	-1		-1				
TRAH				-1			
A_TR	-1						
OVR_	-1						
TRAM	-1						
PAPP			-1	-1	-2		-2
PPPP				-1	-2		-1
TRAF	-1				1		1
OVRX	-1	1					
GRAF	-1						
KEMI				-2			
GODS				-1			
BASP	-1						
PLAS	-1	1					
LAKE	-1	1		1	1		1
TVAT	-1						
OVRK	-1		-1				
PETR	18	-9	-2	23	-11		-11
SMOR			-1	-1			
GUMM	-1						

Table 6.9   (*continued*)

PLSV	-1	1					
PORS	-1				1		1
GLAS							1
TEGE				-1	-1		
CEME			-1	-1	-1		-1
OVRM				-1			
JRN_				-1	-6	1	-4
FERR	-1				3	-1	2
JNGJ	-1	1			11	2	13
META					4	2	6
METV	-1				7	4	11
I_JA	-1	1			11	2	13
METR	-1						1
MSKN	-1	1			1		1
ELMO	-1	1					
TELE	-1	1		1			
HUSH	-1	1		1			
OVRE	-1	1					
VARV	-1						
RALS	-1		-1				
BILA	-1	1		1	2		2
CYKL	-1	1		1			
FLYG	-1		-1				
OVRR	-1						
INST	-1	1					
A_TI	-1						
EL_O				-1	-5		-5
GASV	16	-1			-13		-13
BYGG	-1				1		1
VARU			-1	-1	-2		-2
HOTE	-1				1		1
SAMF				1	-57		-57
POST	-1				1		1
EGNA	-1	1			3		3
FAST	-1				1		1
UPPD	-1				1		1
REPA	-1				2		2
OVRP	-1	1			2		3
TOTAL					-52	6	-47

Table 6.10 Impacts on welfare and aggregate carbon emissions of all scenarios

	Aggregate welfare impact		Aggregate CO_2 emissions		
Scenario	Billion SEK	%	Domestic	Foreign	Global
BENCH			50029.4	11786.3	61815.7
C100	-3.9	-0.3	-52.2	5.6	-46.6
C100V	-4.3	-0.4	-99.0	-2.4	-101.4
C100LS	-4.6	-0.4	-118.7	-11.6	-130.2
N100	-3.9	-0.3	-47.2	5.8	-41.4
N75	-7.8	-0.7	-229.3	12.6	-216.7
NU75	-3.8	-0.3	-180.6	6.4	-174.2

Table 6.11 Detailed carbon tax revenue effects of doubling the carbon tax (scenario C100)

	Benchmark Revenues (billion SEK)				Change in Scenario C100 (billion SEK)			
Sector	STEN	PETR	GASV	TOTAL	STEN	PETR	GASV	TOTAL
JORD	0.496	0.704		1.200	0.495	0.646		1.141
SKOG		0.222		0.222		0.203		0.203
FSKE		0.095		0.095		0.086		0.086
JARN	0.105	0.061		0.165	0.101	0.054		0.155
A_ME	0.013	0.045		0.058	0.014	0.041		0.055
STEN		0.058		0.058		0.047		0.047
SLAK		0.020	0.003	0.022		0.018	0.002	0.020
MEJE		0.019	0.005	0.023		0.017	0.004	0.021
FRUK		0.007	0.009	0.017		0.007	0.009	0.016
FISK		0.002		0.002		0.002		0.002
FETT		0.007	0.003	0.010		0.007	0.002	0.009
KVAR		0.002		0.002		0.001		0.001
BAGE		0.016	0.003	0.020		0.015	0.003	0.019
SOCK	0.009	0.012	0.014	0.035	0.008	0.011	0.013	0.032
CHOK		0.005	0.001	0.005		0.004		0.004
DIVX		0.007	0.001	0.008		0.007		0.007
FODE		0.005	0.001	0.006		0.004	0.002	0.006
DRYC		0.013	0.006	0.019		0.013	0.005	0.018
TOBA				0.001		0.001	0.001	0.002
GARN		0.013	0.001	0.014		0.012	0.002	0.013
TEXT		0.001		0.001		0.001		0.001
TRIK		0.001		0.002		0.002		0.002
OVRT		0.004		0.004		0.003		0.004
BEKL		0.002		0.002		0.002	0.001	0.003
LADE		0.001		0.001		0.001		0.001
S2GV		0.022		0.022		0.021		0.021

Table 6.11 (continued)

TRAH		0.009		0.009		0.008		0.008
A_TR		0.006		0.006		0.006		0.006
OVR_		0.002		0.002		0.002		0.002
TRAM		0.007		0.007		0.006		0.006
PAPP	0.028	0.046		0.074	0.028	0.042		0.070
PPPP		0.107	0.010	0.116		0.097	0.008	0.105
TRAF		0.001		0.001				
PFRP		0.007	0.002	0.009		0.006	0.002	0.008
OVRX	0.001	0.004		0.005		0.004		0.005
GRAF		0.016		0.017		0.015		0.016
KEMI	0.204	0.249	0.001	0.454	0.201	0.226		0.428
GODS	0.045	0.008	0.001	0.054	0.045	0.007	0.001	0.053
BASP	0.003	0.010	0.002	0.016	0.004	0.010	0.002	0.015
PLAS	0.007	0.007	0.002	0.015	0.006	0.006	0.001	0.014
FARG	0.003	0.009	0.001	0.012	0.004	0.007		0.011
LAKE		0.009		0.009		0.008		0.008
TVAT		0.002		0.002		0.001		0.002
OVRK	0.021	0.009	0.003	0.033	0.022	0.008	0.003	0.033
PETR		0.188		0.188		0.123		0.123
SMOR	0.243	0.024	0.002	0.269	0.240	0.023	0.002	0.265
GUMM	0.002	0.004		0.006	0.002	0.004		0.006
PLSV		0.009		0.009		0.008		0.008
PORS		0.004		0.004		0.003		0.003
GLAS		0.024		0.024		0.021		0.021
TEGE		0.004	0.003	0.008		0.005	0.003	0.008
CEME		0.007		0.007		0.007		0.007
OVRM		0.043	0.002	0.045		0.039	0.002	0.041
JRN_	0.145	0.125	0.006	0.275	0.144	0.114	0.005	0.263
FERR	0.003			0.003	0.002	0.001		0.003
JNGJ	0.018	0.003		0.021	0.018	0.003		0.021
META	0.028	0.010	0.002	0.039	0.028	0.008	0.001	0.038
METV		0.007		0.007		0.007		0.007
I_JA	0.013	0.002		0.015	0.013	0.003		0.015
METR	0.002	0.053	0.002	0.057	0.002	0.048	0.002	0.053
MSKN	0.006	0.048	0.002	0.057	0.006	0.045	0.002	0.054
ELMO		0.003		0.003		0.002		0.002
TELE		0.005		0.005		0.006		0.006
HUSH		0.001		0.001		0.001		0.001
OVRE	0.017	0.008		0.024	0.017	0.007		0.023
VARV		0.005	0.001	0.006		0.004		0.005
RALS		0.004		0.004		0.003		0.003
BILA	0.016	0.049	0.007	0.072	0.016	0.045	0.007	0.069
CYKL				0.001		0.001		0.001
FLYG		0.003		0.003		0.003		0.003
OVRR						0.001		0.001
INST		0.004		0.004		0.003		0.003
A_TI		0.003		0.003		0.002		0.002

Table 6.11 (continued)

EL_O		1.156	0.473	1.630		1.060	0.438	1.498
GASV		0.618		0.618		0.517		0.517
BYGG		1.599		1.599		1.467		1.467
VARU		1.572	0.085	1.657		1.430	0.078	1.508
HOTE		0.227	0.022	0.249		0.209	0.020	0.230
SAMF		4.183		4.183		3.809		3.809
POST		0.101		0.101		0.092		0.092
BANK		0.169	0.004	0.174		0.156	0.004	0.160
FAST		0.746	0.037	0.783		0.687	0.034	0.720
UPPD		0.659	0.022	0.681		0.605	0.020	0.625
REPA		0.091		0.091		0.083		0.083
OVRP	0.142	0.481		0.623	0.143	0.445		0.588
TOTAL	1.568	14.096	0.740	16.405	1.559	12.787	0.686	15.032

Table 6.12 Sectoral impact of doubling the carbon tax with a nuclear shutdown (scenario N75)

Sector	IPRICE%	VA%	IMP%	EXP%	CO2_D	
FRUK	-1	1		1	1	
FISK	-2	2		1	1	
FETT	-1	1		1		
KVAR	-1	1				
BAGE	-1	1	-1	1	1	
SOCK		1		-1		
CHOK	-1	2			1	
DIVX	-2	1			1	
FODE	-1	1	-1			
DRYC	-2	2		2	2	
TOBA	-2	2		3	1	
GARN	-1	1		1	1	
TEXT	-2	2	-2	3		
TRIK	-2	2	-1	4		
OVRT	-2	1	-1	1		
BEKL	-2	2		2		
LADE	-2	2		2		
S2GV	-5	1	-4	1	1	
TRAH	-1		-2	-2		
A_TR	-2	1				
OVR	-2	1	-1			
TRAM	-2	2				
PAPP	-1	-7	-8	-8	-33	-2
PPPP	6	-8	4	-12	-35	1
TRAF			-2		-1	1
PFRP	1	1	-1	-1		
OVRX			-1	-2		
GRAF	-1	1	-1		1	
KEMI		-1	-1	-3	-1	
GODS	-1	1	-1	-1		

Table 6.12 (continued)

BASP	-1	1				
PLAS	-1	2	-1	1	1	
FARG	-2	1	-1			
LAKE	-2	5	-1	5	3	
TVAT	-2	2		1		
OVRK	-2	2	-1	2	1	
PETR	17	-8	-2	-22	-11	
SMOR	-1	1	-1	-1		
GUMM	-2	2				
PLSV	-1	2		1	1	
PORS	-1	2	-1	1	2	
GLAS	-1	1			3	1
TEGE	-1		-1	-1	-1	-1
CEME	2	-2	-1	-6	-7	
OVRM	-1		-1	-1	-2	
JRN_	2	-2		-6	-78	4
FERR	2	-4	-2	-8	-124	-13
JNGJ		2	1	-1	24	9
META	1	-1	-1	-3	-36	2
METV	-1	1			11	7
I_JA		2	1		24	7
METR	-1	1	-1		1	
MSKN	-2	2	-1	1	3	
ELMO	-2	3		3		
TELE	-2	3		3	1	
HUSH	-2	3	-1	4		
OVRE	-2	1	-1	1		
VARV	-2	2		1		
RALS	-1	1	-1			
BILA	-2	3		3	6	
CYKL	-2	2	-1	4		
FLYG	-2	2	-1	2	1	
OVRR	-2	2	-1	1		
INST	-2	3		3	1	
A_TI	-1	1				
EL_O	55	-25	1	-42	-5	3
GASV	15	-6			-27	
VATT		1				
BYGG	-2				-3	
VARU	-1	1	-1		1	
HOTE	-2	1			6	
SAMF	-1	1	-1		59	
POST	-2	1	-1	1	5	
BANK	-1	1				
EGNA	-3	3			13	
FAST		1			-1	
UPPD	-2	1	-1	1	5	
REPA	-2	2			8	
OVRP	-2	2		2	11	2
TOTAL					-234	13

Table 6.13 Costs and benefits to Swedes in SEK of doubling the carbon tax (scenario C100)

Household	Average individuals			Average household		
	Benefit	Cost	Per cent	Benefit	Cost	Per cent
S_NC_1	3	415	1	6	415	2
S_NC_2	3	283	1	6	283	2
S_NC_3	3	409	1	6	409	2
S_NC_4	3	345	1	6	345	2
S_C_1	3	226	1	6	521	1
S_C_2	3	431	1	6	1164	1
M_NC_1	3	617		6	1234	1
M_NC_2	3	464	1	6	928	1
M_NC_3	3	653		6	1307	
M_NC_4	3	693		6	1387	
M_1C_1	3	386	1	6	1157	1
M_1C_2	3	448	1	6	1343	
M_1C_3	3	537	1	6	1611	
M_1C_4	3	762		6	2287	
M_2C_1	3	416	1	6	1666	
M_2C_2	3	481	1	6	1924	
M_2C_3	3	602		6	2407	
M_2C_4	3	758		6	3033	
M_3C_1	3	299	1	6	1557	
M_3C_2	3	363	1	6	1887	
M_3C_3	3	461	1	6	2397	
M_3C_4	3	537	1	6	2900	
O_NC_1	3	436	1	6	959	1
O_NC_2	3	418	1	6	1128	1
O_NC_3	3	542	1	6	1571	
O_NC_4	3	562	1	6	1911	
O_C_1	3	348	1	6	1323	
O_C_2	3	320	1	6	1375	
O_C_3	3	456	1	6	1963	
O_C_4	3	569	1	6	2562	
AVE	3	500	1	6	1090	1

REFERENCES

Anderson, K. and Norman, E. (1987), 'Capital Taxation and Neutrality. A Study of Tax Wedges with Special Reference to Sweden', *Lund Economic Studies Number 41*, Department of Economics, University of Lund.

Bergman, L. (1991), 'Tillväxt och miljö', *Bilaga 21 till LU-90*, Finansdepartmentet, Stockholm. (In Swedish: 'Growth and the Environment', Supplement 21 to the Swedish Medium-Term Economic Survey, Treasury of Sweden).

Blackburn, McKinley, Harrison, G. and Rutström, E. (1994), 'Statistical Bias Functions and Informative Hypothetical Surveys', *American Journal of Agricultural Economics*, **76** (5), 1084-8.

Bovenberg, L. and Goulder, L. (1995a), 'Costs of Environmentally Motivated Taxes in the Presence of Other Taxes: General Equilibrium Analyses', *Working Paper No. 5117*, National Bureau of Economic Research, Inc.

Bovenberg, L. and Goulder, L. (1995b), 'Optimal Environmental Taxation in the Presence of Other Taxes: General Equilibrium Analyses', *Unpublished Manuscript*, Department of Economics, Stanford University.

Brooke, A., Kendrick, D. and Meeraus, A. (1992), *GAMS: A User's Guide, Release 2.25*, Danvers, MA., Boyd & Fraser.

Cummings, R., Elliott, S., Harrison, G. and Murphy, J. (1996), 'Are Hypothetical Referenda Incentive Compatible?', *Journal of Political Economy*, **105**, forthcoming.

Cummings, R., Harrison, G. and Rutström, E. (1995), 'Homegrown Values and Hypothetical Surveys: Is the Dichotomous Choice Approach Incentive Compatible?', *American Economic Review*, **85** (1), 260-6.

Dirkse, S. and Ferris, M. (1995), 'The PATH Solver: A Non-Monotone Stabilization Scheme for Mixed Complementarity Problems', *Optimization Methods and Software*, **5**, 123-56.

Goulder, L. (1995a), 'Environmental Taxation and the Double Dividend: A Reader's Guide', *International Tax and Public Finance*, **2**, 157-83.

Goulder, L. (1995b), 'Effects of Carbon Taxes in an Economy with Prior Tax Distortions: An Intertemporal General Equilibrium Analysis', *Journal of Environmental Economics and Management*, **29** (3), 271-97.

Harrison, G. (1994), 'Environmentally Sensitive Industries and an Emerging Mexico', *North American Journal of Economics and Finance*, **4** (1), 109-26.

Harrison, G., Jones, R., Kimbell, L. and Wigle, R. (1993), 'How Robust Is Applied General Equilibrium Analysis?', *Journal of Policy Modeling*, **15** (1), 99-115.

Harrison, G. and Kriström, B. (1995), 'On the interpretation of responses in contingent valuation surveys', in P.-O. Johansson, B. Kriström and K.-G. Mäler (eds), *Current Issues in Environmental Economics,* New York, Manchester University Press.

Harrison, G. and Kriström, B. (1996), 'Carbon Taxes in Sweden', *Final Report to the Skatteväxlingskommittén*, Stockholm, forthcoming.

Harrison, G. and Manning, R. (1987), 'Best Approximate Aggregation of Input-Output Systems', *Journal of the American Statistical Association*, **83**, 1027-31.

Harrison, G.; Rutherford, T. and Tarr, D. (1993), 'Piecemeal Trade Reform in the Partially Liberalized Economy of Turkey', *World Bank Economic Review*, **7**, 191-217.

Harrison, G., Rutherford, T. and Tarr, D. (1994), 'Product Standards, Imperfect Competition, and the Completion of the Market in the European Community', *Policy Research Working Paper* **1293**, International Economics Department, International Trade Division, The World Bank, forthcoming in *Journal of Economic Integration*.

Harrison, G., Rutherford, T. and Tarr, D. (1995), 'Quantifying the Outcome of the Uruguay Round', *Finance & Development*, **32** (4), 38-41.

Harrison, G., Rutherford, T. and Tarr, D. (1996), 'Quantifying the Uruguay Round', in W. Martin and L.A. Winters (eds), *The Uruguay Round and the Developing Countries*, New York, Cambridge University Press.

Harrison, G. and Vinod, H.D. (1992), 'The Sensitivity Analysis of Applied General Equilibrium Models: Completely Randomized Factorial Sampling Designs', *The Review of Economics and Statistics*, **74**, 357-62.

Jorgenson, D. and Wilcoxen, P. (1995), 'Intertemporal Equilibrium Modeling of Energy and Environmental Policies', in P.-O. Johansson, B. Kriström and K.-G. Mäler (eds), *Current Issues in Environmental Economics*, New York, Manchester University Press.

de Melo, J. and Tarr, D. (1992), *General Equilibrium Analysis of U.S. Foreign Trade Policy*, Cambridge, MA, MIT Press.

Nordhaus, W. (1995), 'The Swedish Dilemma: Nuclear Energy *v.* The Environment', *Report to Studieförbundet Näringsliv och Samhälle*, Stockholm.

Perroni, C. and Rutherford, T. (1995a), 'Regular flexibility of nested CES functions', *European Economic Review*, **39**, 335-43.

Perroni, C. and Rutherford, T. (1995b), 'A Comparison of the Performance of Flexible Functional Forms For Use in Applied General Equilibrium Analysis', *Discussion Paper 95-6*, Department of Economics, University of Colorado at Boulder.

Reinert, K.A. and Roland-Holst, D.W. (1992), 'Armington Elasticities for the Manufacturing Sectors of the United States', *Journal of Policy Modeling*, **14** (5), 631-9.

Reinert, K.A. and Shiells, C.R. (1991), 'Trade Substitution Elasticities for Analysis of a North American Free Trade Area', unpublished manuscript, Office of Economics, U.S. International Trade Commission.

Rutherford, T. (1992), 'Applied General Equilibrium Modeling with MPSGE as a GAMS Subsystem', *Economics Working Paper 92-15*, Department of Economics, University of Colorado at Boulder.

Rutherford, T. (1993), 'MILES: a Mixed Inequality and non-Linear Equation Solver', *Economics Working Paper*, Department of Economics, University of Colorado at Boulder.

Rutherford, T. (1995), 'Extensions of GAMS for Complementarity and Variational Problems Arising in Applied Economics', *Journal of Economic Dynamics and Control*, **19** (8), 1299-324.

Rutherford, T., Rutström, E. and Tarr, D. (1994), 'L'Accord de Libre Echange entre le Maroc et la CEE: Une Evaluation Quantitative', *Revue d'Economie du Developpement*, **2**, 97-133.

Statens Offentliga Utvedningar (SOU), (1990), *Sätt Värde på Miljön: Miljöavgifter och andra Ekonomiska Styrmedel* (in Swedish, Final Report from the Commission on Environmental Charges), Stockholm, Norstedts.

Statens Offentliga Utvedningar (SOU), (1994), *Ny Lag om Skatt på Energi: En Teknisk Översyn och EG-anpassning* (in Swedish, Report from the Committee on Energy Taxation, Part 1), Stockholm, Norstedt.

Treasury of Sweden (1995), 'Energi och Miljörelaterade Skatter I Sverige och I

OCED-länderna' (in Swedish, 'Energy and Environmentally Related Taxes in Sweden and the OECD Countries'), unpublished manuscript, Treasury of Sweden, Stockholm.

7   Green Taxes in Sweden: A Partial Equilibrium Analysis of the Carbon Tax and the Tax on Nitrogen in Fertilizers

Runar Brännlund and Ing-Marie Gren

7.1 INTRODUCTION

The purpose of this chapter is twofold. First of all we want to give a brief overview of the development of environmental policy in Sweden. Secondly, we attempt to analyse the impact from the tax on the carbon content in fossil fuels, hereafter called the carbon dioxide tax (CO_2 tax), and the tax on nitrogen in fertilizers.

Our interest in this issue is founded on the belief of the great importance in the discussion of a green tax reform to have, at least crude, estimates of what the impact of individual taxes might be. Specifically there are two different, but related, impacts which are of great importance. The first one is of course the environmental effects from eco taxes. The second one is the effects from a fiscal point of view. Obviously, environmental effects and fiscal effects are related. If a tax increase gives rise to a substantial positive environmental effect in terms of reduced emissions, then we will have, by definition, a substantial erosion of the tax base. No emissions, no eco tax revenues. Although this is obvious, it is nevertheless of great importance to have this relation in mind when analysing green tax reforms since the discussion around green tax reforms has focused on revenue neutral reforms.

The idea behind revenue neutral reforms is to use revenues from eco taxes to finance cuts in other taxes which are viewed as distortionary. The belief is then that we will obtain a double dividend. The first dividend is due to the positive environmental effect, and the second dividend is the efficiency gain due to lower distortionary taxes. Thus, the importance of an analysis of the environmental and tax erosion effects from green taxes should be quite apparent[1]. The subject of analysis, the CO_2 tax and the tax on nitrogen, can be motivated by two reasons. First of all, as is shown in Chapter 3 in this volume, the CO_2 tax is by far the most important Swedish eco tax when it comes to tax revenues. The contribution from the CO_2 tax to total revenues from 'pure' environmental taxes is more than 90 per cent. Thus, in a green tax reform in which one of the aims is to reduce some other tax, the CO_2 tax is the only eco tax which can give a sustainable and significant contribution. In addition, the CO_2 tax is one of the few true emission taxes in Sweden. The interest for the tax on nitrogen in fertilizers is due to the specific environmental problem caused by the use of nitrogen fertilizers in Swedish agriculture. In contrast to CO_2 emissions the source of emissions is of great importance when we consider the environmental problem of nitrogen emissions. Total damage caused by nitrogen emissions will thus depend on the location of emission sources. This in turn may call for a quite different policy than in the case of CO_2 emissions.

The rest of the chapter is structured in the following way. Section 2 is devoted to the institutional setting concerning environmental policy in Sweden. Here we will outline the general structure as well as give an overview of the areas which are currently subject to eco taxes. A partial equilibrium econometric analysis of the demand for fossil fuels and other energy goods as well as nitrogen is presented in Section 3. The analysis is focused on the manufacturing sector, the private household sector and the agricultural sector. Here we also present some simulations of CO_2 tax changes and changes of the nitrogen tax. Finally, in Section 4 we give some concluding remarks.

7.2 ENVIRONMENTAL POLICY IN SWEDEN

In this section we make an attempt to shed some light on how Swedish environmental policy has evolved over the years in response to changing environmental problems as well as changing priorities. By and large, it is an ideal time to make an assessment of this kind, because we have witnessed dramatic changes, both in terms of the underlying problems and of environmental policy itself. Our analysis covers the past, the present and, in a sense, the future.

Environmental problems are not a new phenomenon. Every founding of a city, each industrial activity from the earliest human settlements and onwards have created negative effects on the surrounding environment or on man's

---

1 For a discussion of the double dividend issue and the pitfalls to look out for, we refer to Oates (1995), Bovenberg and Goulder (1996), and the contribution by David Starrett in this volume.

health and well-being. These negative effects have been accepted as long as they have not meant acute health problems. When one ponders the fact that Sweden's population is roughly that of Paris and that the country is about the size of France, one may wonder why Sweden has any environmental problems at all. Indeed, factories are widely dispersed, urban areas are small in international comparison and the country is well-endowed with fresh water. In addition, a number of lakes/rivers in major cities are now swimable and may even provide excellent hunting grounds for fishermen, as is the case in the city-kernel of Stockholm. In light of the above, an account of environmental problems and environmental policy in Sweden may appear to be rather picayune and uninteresting. In order to show that this is not necessarily the case, we begin by recapitulating some essentials of modern environmental history.

The early environmental problems were usually relatively local in character. They were, as in many other countries, a product of industrialisation and urbanisation. Local environmental problems became most accentuated in the form of water and air pollution in and around the major cities or in the vicinity of larger industries. As much as the forest industry and the metal-based industry contributed to the prosperity of the country, they were also responsible for a major part of the emissions from industrial sources. In urban areas, air pollution from heating houses and water pollution from the release of untreated waste water were major health hazards.

The local environmental problems have, to a large extent, been eliminated. For example, the levels of sulphur dioxide in cities have been reduced to 20-40 per cent of those levels that existed 20 years ago. Sulphur dioxide concentrations are, today, generally well below the guidelines and planning goals laid down by the Swedish National Environmental Protection Agency. Indeed, it is now difficult to find any detrimental health effects from local pollution.

Local water pollution mimics the history of local air pollution quite closely. In many cities it was not possible to bathe outdoors during the greater part of this century, because of the release of untreated waste water directly into water courses or the sea. Today, through the development of municipal waste water treatment plants, the water is now fit for bathing even in the central part of Stockholm.

Some local environmental problems do remain. Traffic in densely populated areas and residuals from agriculture in the form of air and water pollution are two major challenges for the current policy. Thus, while sulphur emissions have diminished over time, nitrogen emissions have been fairly stable or have increased.

During the latter part of the 1960s, a series of research findings emerged which indicated that air pollution was not just a local problem, but could be transported from one country to another. Further research showed that many pollution problems were common to the whole of Europe or at least to a large part of the European continent. Sulphur and acid emissions attracted most of the attention. In Sweden, it was Svante Odén's compilation of changes in the pH values in precipitation and surface water from large parts of Europe and C. Brosset's measurement of pollutants along the Swedish south and west coasts, which revealed that acidity was a transboundary problem. It was shown that pollutants were transported to a considerable extent over national boundaries.

While sulphur has received a large amount of attention since the compilations of Odén and Brossett, research subsequently revealed that long distance transportation was a phenomenon that did not apply just to sulphur; also, nitrates, photochemical oxidants, heavy metals, and persistent organic material could be transported in a way analogous to that for sulphur.

The observations by Odén and others were quickly followed by research findings that demonstrated detrimental effects of sulphur on fish, and on human health. For example, in the early 1980s, 16 000 of Sweden's 85 000 lakes were acidified severely; sensitive species had decreased substantially or died out. An extensive liming programme has prevented the death of most forms of life in 6 000 of those lakes. It should be noted, however, that several of the lakes that were considered damaged by anthropogenic emissions are now considered to be naturally acidified.

While sulphur emissions in Sweden have decreased substantially, sulphur deposition still exceeds the critical amount. According to the government bill of 1991, sulphur deposition must be decreased by about 75 per cent of the 1980 level in the south-western parts of Sweden to bring depositions below the critical amount. Such a goal is complicated by the fact that emissions from foreign and diffuse sources accounted for about 90 per cent of sulphur deposition in Sweden in 1985.

The sulphur case explains why one of the main issues in current policy today is to foster international cooperation. The 1979 Convention on Long-Range Transboundary Air Pollution is a forum for European cooperation. A number of binding Protocols have also been developed under the 1979 Geneva convention. For example, the 1985 Sulphur Protocol established a minimum 30 per cent reduction of sulphur emissions between 1980 and 1993.

At the end of the 1970s, the international problems in the marine environment became increasingly apparent. Eutrophication and pollution in the marine environment began to appear more and more as regional problems. This applied to both the Baltic Sea and the North Sea. The large-scale pollution of the oceans during the 1980s became an ever-increasing problem, one that has led to the drawing up of international plans of action for both of the above-mentioned seas.

The risk of a global increase in temperature as a consequence of the increased emissions of carbon dioxide were pointed out 100 years ago by the Swedish chemist (and Nobel-laureate) Svante Arrhenius. The more serious alarms concerning a global effect on the earth's climate came first during the 1970s and have been further accentuated in the past decade. It was, however, first through the discovery of a significantly quicker breakdown than expected of the stratosphere's ozone layer over the Antarctic that global atmospheric pollution issues appeared on the agenda in international negotiations. A contributing factor was also the coverage these questions received in the Brundtland Report. One important feature of the current Swedish policy is to stabilize carbon dioxide emissions by the year 2000 to the 1990 level.

The organizational arrangement of environmental policy in Sweden is as follows. At government level, the Ministry of the Environment is responsible for matters relating to environmental policy. The EPA (Naturvårdsverket) is the central administrative authority and deals with matters such as air and water pollution control, noise abatement, and management of natural resources. At the regional level, the 24 county administrations are the regional supervisory authorities under the Environment Protection Act and the Health Protection Act. Together with the Labour Inspectorate they are also the supervisory authority under the Act on Chemical Products. The 284 municipalities are responsible for local environmental protection. Here, the municipal board for environmental protection and health and the building boards have important functions.

With regard to the general construction of its control system for environmental protection, Sweden belongs to a north European model. It is characterised by individualised non-transferrable permits to sources and the Best-Available-Control-Technology (BACT) principle. Sweden has utilized guidelines for air quality and applied general rules for assessing water quality. In the United States, and increasingly so in European countries, there exist explicit standards for environmental quality. A recent Swedish commission has investigated the feasibility of switching to this model. Changes in current environmental laws are not expected before 1997, however, and the process is further complicated by the as yet unclear effects of a Swedish entry into the European Union.

One of the most important issues in recent Swedish policy has been whether Sweden should enter the European Union. An advisory referendum held on 13 November 1994, resulted in a 52-47 win for the proponents of joining. As a result, Sweden has been a member of the Union since January, 1995. It is not clear, at least not at the time of writing, what kinds of restrictions - if any - there will be on the possibilities of pursuing an independent environmental policy. On the one hand, current Union policy is based on minimum requirements, which means that a member country has an option to use a stricter policy. On the other hand, it is difficult, if not impossible, to block imports of goods that have been approved in another country. For example, a country may have laws that restrict/forbid the use of a certain chemical, but it may not be able to prevent import of goods containing this chemical. Membership in the European Union does not prevent country-specific environmental policies *de jure*, but it may make a deviation from Union policy impossible *de facto*.

There are at least two factors that complicate judgements about how autonomous Sweden's environmental policy is going to be. First, Sweden has been guaranteed the right to keep all present environmental laws until the renegotiations that follow about two years after entry. It is, of course, impossible to predict the outcome of such negotiations at this juncture. Second, any member country can appeal to the Supreme Court of the Union, should there be conflicting views about such issues as, trade union rules and country-specific environmental goals. If it can be shown that the sole purpose of a certain law or prohibition is to protect the life and health of the country's citizens, then the court can grant the right to block import of certain goods to the appealing country, provided the law or prohibition is not considered part of a trade war.

Economic instruments in environmental policy have only very recently been generally accepted as viable instruments in Sweden. In the 1970s, large subsidies were given to firms and local governments to facilitate and speed up environmental protection measures. In particular, municipal waste water treatment plants were developed and extended during this period. This subsidisation scheme explains a major part of the substantial improvements in local environmental quality. Subsidies play only a minor role today. Subsidies exist for the development of new technology, subsidies for liming of lakes, and a subsidy for the preservation of the cultural landscape.

A major shift in emphasis came with the appointment of the Commission of Environmental Charges in 1988. It was part of a major tax reform. A total of SEK 19 000 million was being transferred from income tax to environmental and energy taxes. The commission produced a large number of proposals in its interim reports (SOU 1989;21, SOU 1989;83) and in its final report (SOU 1990;59). The commission was to analyse the scope for using economic measures in environmental policy on a large scale. Some of the proposals were accepted by the parliament, and a number of environmental charges came into play on 1 January 1991. Table 3.2 in Chapter 3 lists the most important environmental taxes in current use.

By far the most important environmental tax, at least from a fiscal point of view, is the tax on CO_2 that was introduced on 1 January 1991. The current rate is 0.37 SEK/kg CO_2, which corresponds to approximately 200 USD per ton of carbon. The manufacturing industry, however, have a reduced rate amounting to 25 per cent of the general level. In total the revenues from the CO_2 tax amounts to approximately 13 billion SEK, or approximately 1.7

billion USD. This should be compared with the total revenues from all energy and environmental related taxes which amounts to 52 billion SEK, or roughly 7 billion USD.

7.3 A PARTIAL EQUILIBRIUM ANALYSIS OF GREEN TAXES

As mentioned before in Chapter 3 of this volume, one of the objectives for the Swedish Green Tax Commission has been to assess whether environmentally related taxes have been efficient or not, in terms of reducing the negative load on the environment. In this section we will report some of the findings of this work. It should be pointed out that it is a difficult task to make such an assessment. The main reason for this difficulty is that many of the green taxes in use were introduced quite recently, which means that we have very little experience of the effects, especially the long-run effects. However, in spite of this we claim that there is some scope for such an assessment. Suppose that a tax, such as the CO_2 tax, or the sulphur tax, is equivalent to a consumer price increase on fossil fuels. Thus, in principle, if we know how different users is changing its behaviour in response to price changes, then we also can tell what the effects will be of a specific change in the tax. One way to evaluate the effects of such eco-taxes amounts in principle to an estimation of price elasticities. If the price elasticity for, say, petroleum is negative, then we know that a higher consumer price (everything else unchanged) leads to lower consumption, and hence lower emissions of various substances such as CO_2. Thus, if a tax increase on fossil fuels leads to an increase in the consumer price by the same amount, which is a reasonable assumption for a country like Sweden, then the tax will have the intended effect.

In order to analyse the sensitivity to price changes we employ a partial equilibrium framework. In this case this means that we will analyse the industry, the household sector, and the agriculture sector separately. The analysis is partial in the sense that all prices are assumed to be exogenous to all agents. This is of course a simplification of the real world, but one might view it as a first order approximation. A similar general equilibrium analysis can be found in the contribution by Harrison and Kriström in this volume, and Harrison and Kriström (1997).

7.3.1 The Industry

In this study the industry is disaggregated into 16 manufacturing sectors, and each manufacturing sector is assumed to produce one good (y) using labour (x_l), fossil fuels (x_f), electricity (x_e) and capital (x_K) as inputs. The underlying assumption behind the derivation of goods supply and input demand is that each firm seeks to maximize its profits. Formally the profit from the industry is written as:

$$\pi^i = p_y^i y^i - \sum_j p_j^i x_j^i, \quad i = 1, \ldots, 16 \quad j = l, f, e, K \tag{7.1}$$

where p_j^i is the price of input j in sector i. The model is viewed as a short run model which means that capital is assumed to be fixed in the short run. The short run profit function is then obtained by maximizing profits for each industry with respect to output and variable inputs:

$$\pi^i = \pi^i(p_y^i, p_l^i, p_f^i, p_e^i, x_K^i) \tag{7.2}$$

The derived supply and demand functions are obtained by applying Hotelling's lemma:

$$\frac{\partial \pi^i}{\partial p_y} = y^i = y^i(\underset{+}{p_y^i}, \underset{?}{p_l^i}, \underset{?}{p_e^i}, \underset{?}{p_f^i}, \underset{?}{x^i}) \tag{7.3i}$$

$$-\frac{\partial \pi^i}{\partial p_l^i} = x_l^i = x_l^i(\underset{?}{p_y^i}, \underset{-}{p_l^i}, \underset{?}{p_e^i}, \underset{?}{p_f^i}, \underset{?}{x^i}) \tag{7.3ii}$$

$$-\frac{\partial \pi^i}{\partial p_e^i} = x_e^i = x_e^i(\underset{?}{p_y^i}, \underset{?}{p_l^i}, \underset{-}{p_e^i}, \underset{?}{p_f^i}, \underset{?}{x^i}) \tag{7.3iii}$$

$$-\frac{\partial \pi^i}{\partial p_f^i} = x_f^i = x_f^i(\underset{?}{p_y^i}, \underset{?}{p_l^i}, \underset{?}{p_e^i}, \underset{-}{p_f^i}, \underset{?}{x^i}) \tag{7.3iv}$$

The sign under the argument is the expected sign of the partial derivative.

To estimate the parameters in the profit functions, we need to parameterize the model. This is done by assuming that the technology in each industry can be represented by a restricted Generalized Leontief (GL) profit function, which is a second order differential approximation of any arbitrary profit function.

$$\pi^i = \left[\sum_m \sum_n \beta_{mn} p_m^{i\,1/2} p_n^{i\,1/2} + \sum_m \beta_{mt} p_m T + \right.$$

$$\left. \sum_j \sum_m \beta_{jm} D_j p_m + \sum_j \sum_m \beta_{jmt} D_j T p_m \right] \cdot x_K$$

$$m = y, l, e, f$$
$$n = y, l, e, f$$
$$i = 1, \dots 16 \qquad\qquad (7.4)$$
$$j = 2, \dots, 16$$

where T is a time trend representing technological change, and D_i is a sector specific dummy variable which takes the value of one if the observation belonging to the $j{:}th$ sector and zero otherwise. Given that sector, or industry, 1 and 2 are facing the same input and output prices, profits will in general differ, i.e.,

$$\pi^1 - \pi^2 = -\sum_m \beta_{2m} p_m - \sum_m \beta_{2mt} T p_m \qquad\qquad (7.5)$$

The empirical specification in (7.4) is employed on yearly data collected from SCB, Industry and NUCOMDAT. The data set covers the period 1974-93 for 16 different manufacturing sectors. Production, y, is measured as sales value minus costs for intermediate materials, and the price of y is the producer price index in each sector. Labour, x_l, and wages, p_l, are measured as the number of employed in each sector and the total labour cost per worker respectively. Electricity input, x_e, is measured as millions of MWh used in each sector. The price of electricity, p_e, is measured as the ratio between total outlays on electricity and total use. Input of fuels, x_f, are equal to consumption of various oil and coal products in physical units. The corresponding price is calculated by dividing total costs for oil and coal by total quantity used. Capital, finally, is an index for the capital stock in each sector in fixed prices collected from the National Accounts.

The system of supply and demand equations, resulting from applying Hotelling's lemma on (7.4), is estimated as a system of Seemingly Unrelated system (SURE). The resulting price elasticities are presented in Table 7.1.[2]

Table 7.1 should be read in the following way. If the price of fossil fuels increases by 10 per cent, the demand for fossil fuels decreases by 3.2 per

---

2 For a more detailed description of the model, see Report No 4 in SOU 1997:11.

Green Taxes

Table 7.1   *Average own price and cross price elasticities for the Swedish*
manufacturing industry, (t-values within parenthesis)

	Output price	Wage	Electricity price	Fossil fuel price
Goods supply	0.12	-0.08	-0.03	-0.01
	(4.34)	(-2.99)	(-9.42)	(-3.05)
Labour demand	0.14	-0.13	-0.02	0.008
	(2.99)	(-2.83)	(-2.66)	(0.97)
Electricity demand	0.64	-0.22	-0.26	-0.16
	(9.42)	(-2.66)	(-2.76)	(-3.10)
Fossil fuel demand	0.40	0.12	-0.19	-0.32
	(3.06)	(0.97)	(-3.10)	(-4.68)

cent. In addition, this will lead to a 1.6 per cent decrease of electricity demand, and an almost unchanged demand for labour. Output will according to these estimates decrease by 0.1 per cent. In other words, the effects are very small, suggesting that taxes on oil have a rather small impact on the environment. It should be pointed out that these elasticities should be interpreted as short run elasticities since the capital stock is treated as fixed. In the long run we should expect that a price change do have an effect on capital formation in the industry. Thus we expect that the industry is more sensitive to price changes in the long run.

To conclude we have found that the industry reacts to price changes the way we would expect. All own-price demand elasticities are negative. This means that higher prices on fossil fuels, because of higher CO_2 or sulphur taxes, have a negative effect on demand for fossil fuels. The short run effects are, however, small. The latter implies that we can't expect any large environmental effects, at least in the short run, by increasing the CO_2 tax further. On the other hand this also implies that the tax base is fairly stable in the short run. Suppose, for example, that the policy makers decide that the industry should cut down its emissions of CO_2 by 25 per cent. To achieve this goal a 250 per cent tax increase from today's level would achieve this. This would amount to a tax increase from today's 0.09 SEK/kg CO_2 to approximately 0.34 SEK per kilo, which is equivalent to a 23 per cent increase of the oil price.

It should be stressed that the figures in Table 7.1 represent short run effects. In the long run, when capital is variable, one can expect considerably higher elasticities. The results presented here are, however, quite coherent with the results from similar studies where also the long run effects are estimated. In a study by Walfridsson och Hjalmarsson (1991) the own price elasticity for electricity in the Swedish manufacturing sector is estimated to -0.03 in the short run and -0.14 in the long run. The corresponding figures for fossil fuels are -0.08 and -0.37. They are in other words close to the results presented here. In an earlier study Dargay (1983) estimated the long run own price elasticity for electricity and fuels to -0.21 and -0.60 respectively.

7.3.2 The Household Sector

The major part of energy consumption within the household sector in Sweden is through consumption of transport and heating of houses. About 10 per cent of total household expenditure on non-durable goods are allocated to expenditures on transport. Expenditures on energy for heating are of the same magnitude. Thus it should be quite clear that the household sector has to be considered when it comes to an analysis of energy and/or environmentally related taxes.

Household behaviour in this study is analysed through a system of demand functions, describing how the demand for a specific good changes when the price of some good, or the income, changes. The system of demand functions is derived by assuming utility maximizing households. The model used here is a 'two-stage budgeting' model which uses aggregate data from the national accounts. In the first stage the household determines, given its total budget, how much to spend on transport, heating and other goods. Given this choice the household in the second stage allocates resources within each group. For example, given a specific amount of money to be spent on transport, the household determines, in the second stage how much should be allocated to expenditures on petroleum, public transport and other means of transport (taxi, train, airplane, etc.). In the same manner the household determines in the second stage how to use its budget for heating. In this case the household can choose between electricity, oil or district heating.

Formally it is assumed that the household expenditures on non-durable commodities are distributed according to an 'Almost Ideal Demand System' (AIDS).[3] This means that the expenditures on a specific commodity, or group of commodities, in relation to total expenditures, can be written as:

$$w_i = \alpha_i + \sum_j \gamma_{ij} \ln p_j + \beta_i \ln(y / P) + \varepsilon_i \qquad (7.6)$$

where w_i is commodity i:s share of total expenditures, p_j is a price index for commodity j, P is the 'consumer price index', y is income which in this case equals total expenditures, and ε_i is the random element. The parameters to be estimated are then α, β and γ.

---

3   See Deaton and Muellbauer (1980).

The consumer price index, P, is determined simultaneously with the expenditure shares, but here we use, as an approximation, Stone's linear price index which can be written as:

$$P = \prod_j p_j^{w_j}$$

or

$$\ln P = \sum_j w_j \ln p_j \qquad (7.7)$$

which simply means that the price level on non-durable goods equals a weighted average of all commodity prices where the weight equals the expenditure share of the commodity.

In this specific case with two-stage budgeting we will get three different sets of equations (7.6). In the first set we get the expenditure shares for each group of commodities, i.e., *transport*, *heating*, and *other goods*. In this first set 'income', y, equals total expenditure on non-durable goods. In the second set of equations we have the expenditure shares for the commodities within transports, i.e., expenditure shares for *petroleum*, *public transport*, and *other transport* in relation to total expenditure on transport. Thus, in this second set y equals total expenditure on transport and P equals a price index on transport. The third set, finally, gives the expenditure share for commodities used for heating purposes. Thus we have that y in this last set equals total expenditure on *electricity*, *oil*, and *district heating*, and P is a price index on heating.

In order to fulfil the requirements demanded by consumer theory the equation system must fulfil certain conditions. The first is that the sum of the expenditure shares equals one, i.e., nothing is saved. For this to influence we must have that:

$$\sum_i \alpha_i = 1, \sum_i \beta_i = \sum_i \gamma_{ij} = 0 . \qquad (7.8)$$

Furthermore we impose the condition of no 'money illusion', which means that the demand functions are homogenous of degree 0 in all prices and income. This can be expressed as:

$$\sum_j \gamma_{ij} = 0 . \qquad (7.9)$$

Finally we impose symmetry, i.e.,

$$\gamma_{ij} = \gamma_{ji} \qquad (7.10)$$

Given these restrictions the income elasticities can be calculated as:

$$E_i = 1 + \frac{\beta_i}{w_i} \qquad (7.11)$$

while the uncompensated price elasticities are:

$$e_{ij} = \frac{\gamma_{ij} - \beta_i w_j}{w_i} - \delta_{ij} \qquad (7.12)$$

where

$$\delta_{ij} = 1 \quad if \quad i = j$$
$$\delta_{ij} = 0 \quad if \quad i \neq j$$

The two-stage budgeting model does in this case imply three different sets of equation systems, which in principle can be estimated separately. However, since all three sets are derived from the same utility function efficiency can be gained if the whole system is estimated simultaneously. The method employed here is SURE (seemingly unrelated system) with all the restrictions implied by equations (7.8) to (7.10). The data used in the estimation process are aggregated time-series data for private consumption.

The data set, which are collected from the Swedish National Accounts, are quarterly data spanning over the period 1981 to 1994. Seasonal dummies are used to control seasonal variation.

The results from the estimations are shown in Table 7.2.

The results in Table 7.2 show that most of the estimated parameters are significantly different from zero and that the degree of explanation (R^2) is good. An exception, though, is the equation for the expenditure share for oil within the heating group.

The results in Table 7.2 are used to calculate income and price elasticities for the demand of the various goods according to equations (7.11) and (7.12). The elasticities, which are displayed in Table 7.3, are evaluated for the year of 1994.

Table 7.2 Estimation results of private consumption[4]

			Total consumption				
	Constant	p_t	p_h	p_{og}	(y_c/p_c)	R^2	DW
w_t	0.044	0.0790	-0.0018	-0.0772	0.0054	0.98	1.60
	(1.81)	(13.48)	(-0.41)	(-27.84)	(1.60)		
w_h	0.191	-0.0018	0.0583	-0.0565	-0.0146	0.92	1.52
	(3.00)	(-0.41)	(9.23)	(-10.49)	(-1.64)		
w_{og}	0.765	-0.0772	-0.0565	0.1337	0.0091		
	(12.16)	(-27.84)	(-10.49	(23.91)	(1.04)		
			Within transport				
	Constant	p_g	p_{pt}	p_{ot}	(y_t/p_t)	R^2	DW
w_g	1.134	0.1589	-0.1100	-0.0488	-0.1094	0.94	1.95
	(10.71)	(12.00)	(-9.96)	(-5.35)	(-4.87)		
w_{pt}	0.7020	-0.1100	0.1105	-0.0005	-0.1027	0.95	1.40
	(6.47)	(-9.96)	(8.22)	(-0.06)	(-4.42)		
w_{ot}	-0.835	-0.0488	-0.0005	0.0493	0.2121		
	(-8.19)	(-5.35)	(-0.06)	(4.85)	(9.73)		
			Within heating				
	Constant	p_{el}	p_{oil}	p_{dh}	(y_h/p_h)	R^2	DW
w_{el}	-1.050	0.2617	-0.0932	-0.1685	0.3340	0.62	1.20
	(-3.07)	(6.87)	(-2.44)	(-7.28)	(4.64)		
w_{oil}	3.088	-0.0932	0.1219	-0.0287	-0.6092	0.17	1.35
	(7.64)	(-2.44)	(2.57)	(-1.63)	(-7.17)		
w_{dh}	-1.038	-0.1685	-0.0287	0.1972	0.2753		
	(-6.78)	(-7.28)	(-1.63)	(9.65)	(8.56)		

w_i = expenditure share for group i.
p_i = price of group i.
$i = t, h, og, c$.
t = transport, h = heating, og = other goods, c = total consumption.
w_j = expenditure share for commodity j *within* the corresponding group.
p_j = price of commodity j.

Within transport: $j = g, pt, ot$
g = petroleum, pt = public transport, ot = other transport.

Within heating: $j = el, oil, dh$
el = electricity, oil = oil, dh = district heating.

---

4 All prices and incomes are in natural logarithms.

*Table 7.3   Price and income elasticities for private consumption,
evaluated at 1994 consumption and price levels*

	Price						
Consump-tion	Petroleum	Public trans-port	Other travels	Electri-city	Oil	District heating	Other goods
Petroleum	-0.12	-0.002	-0.002	-0.01	-0.006	-0.008	-0.70
Public transport	-0.005	-0.25	-0.001	-0.01	-0.004	-0.004	-0.41
Other transport	-0.02	-0.007	-0.56	-0.05	-0.02	-0.02	-1.91
Electricity	-0.02	-0.008	-0.006	-0.09	-0.04	-0.04	-0.85
Oil	0.03	0.01	0.008	0.14	-0.19	0.06	1.09
District heating	-0.03		-0.009	-0.15	-0.05	0.00	-1.14
Other goods	-0.06	-0.02	-0.01	-0.03	-0.01	-0.02	-0.72

Income elasticities. Private consumption		
Transport	Heating	Other goods
1.05	0.77	1.01
Petroleum	Public transport	Other transpors
0.83	0.49	2.28
Electricity	Oil	District heating
1.63	-2.09	2.19

The results in Table 7.3 show that all own-price elasticities have a negative sign. In other words, a price increase of one specific good has a negative effect on consumption of the same good. It should also be noted that the own-price elasticities are between 0 and -1 for all goods, which implies that a higher price of one good increases its budget share in spite of lower consumption of that good.

If the price on petroleum increases by 10 per cent, everything else remaining unchanged, then petroleum consumption, according to the results, decreases with approximately 1.2 per cent. The corresponding figure for oil used for heating purposes is 1.9 per cent. A 100 per cent increase of the Swedish CO_2 tax, from 0.37 to 0.74 SEK/kg implies that the consumer price on petroleum increases by approximately 13 per cent, while the oil price for heating increases by 31 per cent. The direct effect on petroleum and oil consumption of such a tax change will be a decrease by 1.6 per cent and 6 per cent respectively. The conclusion is that taxes, such as CO_2 and sulphur tax, have the intended effect in the sense that a tax increase lowers consumption of fossil fuels.

To conclude we have found that taxes on energy, which are part of private consumption, may be very efficient from a fiscal point of view, at least in the short run. In other words, such taxes will generate stable tax revenues, at least in the short and medium term perspective. On the other hand, if the objective for taxation is to reach a specified environmental target, then it should be realised that an ambitious target calls for dramatic changes of the corresponding taxes.

The income elasticities in Table 7.3 can be interpreted in the following way. If income, or more precisely total expenditure, increases by 1 per cent, then demand for transport increases by 1.05 per cent. The corresponding figures for heating and other goods are 0.77 per cent and 1.01 per cent respectively. One interpretation of these figures is that transport and other goods are 'normal goods', i.e., if income increases then consumption of transport and other goods will increase by the same proportion. Heating, on the other hand, seems to be a necessary good since a 1 per cent increase in income leads to less than 1 per cent increase in heating consumption. It can also be seen that a 1 per cent increase in the expenditure on transport will lead to a 0.83 per cent increase of petroleum consumption, a 0.49 per cent increase in public transport, and an increase of other travels by 2.29 per cent. This means that petroleum and public transport seem to be necessary goods in the households transport budget, while other travels is a luxury good. Within the heating group it is found that electricity and district heating are luxury goods, while oil seems to be inferior. This would imply that an income growth over time creates a substantial substitution from oil to electricity and district heating. One explanation to this latter result is that newer houses have either district heating or electricity as the primary heating source. As income grows, more people substitute from old oil heated houses to newer houses with electricity or district heating.

In conclusion we have found that higher incomes will lead to a proportionally equal increase in the consumption of transport and other goods, while energy used for heating purposes will increase less than the increase in income. One implication of this is that energy intensity tends to decrease with economic growth.

The model which has been used here differs from the majority of Swedish empirical energy demand studies. Most studies in this area have been treating petroleum demand separately, without taking into account the interactions between petroleum demand and the demand for other goods. A typical specification of petroleum demand (see Franzén and Sterner (1990), Sterner and Dahl (1991), and Franzén (1994)) is that petroleum demand in a specific country is a function of GDP and the real consumer price of petroleum. Long run effects are, in these models, usually estimated by including lagged consumption as a dependent variable. The drawback with these models is of course that there is no explicit relation between petroleum demand and demand for other goods. In the model used in this chapter this relation exists since we take the budget constraint into account explicitly. The results from most of these models do however conform quite well with the results presented here concerning the own price elasticity for petroleum demand. In Franzén and Sterner (1990), for example the short run elasticity is estimated between -0.21 and -0.13, and in the long run between -0.45 and -0.21.

Simulations of CO_2 tax changes

The private consumption model gives an excellent opportunity to simulate the effects of various tax reforms. An increase in the carbon dioxide tax, for example, will have an effect on not only the petroleum and oil prices, but on essentially all goods we consume. What the effect will be on different commodity prices depends to a large extent on the commodities fossil fuel content. This in turn means that it does not suffice to use the own price elasticities in order to evaluate the effects of a carbon dioxide tax increase. In addition we have to take into account all cross-price effects. An increase of the carbon dioxide tax will, for example, lead to higher consumer prices for petroleum, but probably also to higher prices of public transport and other travel since fossil fuels are an important input in the production of these goods. In addition, a higher carbon dioxide tax implies higher heating prices through higher prices of oil and higher production costs for district heating.

Two scenarios will be presented here. The first one, denoted C100, includes a 100 per cent increase of the carbon dioxide tax without any tax replacement. The second simulation, denoted C100VAT, is a 100 per cent increase of the carbon dioxide tax supplemented with a revenue neutral reduction in the value added tax (VAT).[5] The model is calibrated to the 1994 level of private consumption. The tax rates used, however, are those valid for 1995. Taxes which are considered here are the VAT and excise taxes on energy. This means that we disregard taxes on alcohol and tobacco.

How taxes on energy will affect the demand for the goods in which energy is an input depends critically on two things. The first thing is cost share for energy in the final product, and the second is the possibility to shift the tax burden forward onto the consumers. Concerning 'other goods' we assume that the energy cost share is small and that domestic producers competes with equivalent imported goods, which means the tax cannot be shifted forward. Concerning public transports, 'other travel', and district heating, we assume the opposite, i.e., no import substitutes and a rather high cost share for

---

5   The VAT is 12 per cent on public transport and 25 per cent on other goods. In C100VAT the VAT on public transport is unchanged.

energy. This in turn means that the consumer price will depend on the tax level.

The results of the simulations are reported in Table 7.4.

Table 7.4   Effects of a 100% increase of the Swedish carbon dioxide tax

	Price change		Change in private consumption	
	C100	C100VAT	C100	C100VAT
Private consumption	1.4	0.0		
Transports	10.0	9.1	-2.0	-0.3
Heating	6.0	4.7	-1.5	-0.1
Other goods	0.0	-1.5	-1.3	0.1
Petroleum	13.0	11.0	-2.1	-1.0
Public transports	5.0	5.0	0.1	0.5
Other transports	8.0	6.2	-3.4	0.4
Electricity	0.0	-1.5	-2.2	-0.3
Oil	31.0	29.3	0.09	-1.8
District heating	6.0	4.3	-1.2	1.4

C100   100% increase of CO_2 tax without tax revenue recycling.
C100VAT   100% increase of CO_2 tax with a revenue neutral VAT cut.

In Table 7.4 we see that C100 will lead to an increase of the overall consumer price by approximately 1.4 per cent. The price of transport will increase by 10 per cent, while the price for heating increases by 6 per cent. In other words, transport becomes relatively expensive, compared to other goods. The reason for this is, of course, that transport is relatively fossil fuel intensive.

The price increase for transport is mainly driven by the price increase of petroleum, which is approximately 13 per cent. That the price of public transport and other travel increases less than the price on petroleum depends on the fact that these services are less carbon intensive then petroleum. With heating it can be seen that the price of oil will increase by 31 per cent. This high figure is due to the fact that the initial total tax on oil is considerably lower than the total tax on petroleum.

Concerning consumption changes it is found, as expected, that the largest change occurs within the transport sector. According to Table 7.4, transport consumption decrease by approximately 2 per cent in scenario C100, while heating and consumption of 'other goods' decreases by 1.5 per cent and 1.3

per cent respectively. That the consumption of 'other goods' drops might at first sight seem peculiar since 'other goods' have become relatively less expensive. The explanation is the rise of the general price level, which is equivalent to a drop in real income. This in turn will have a negative effect on consumption of all goods, including 'other goods'.

When it comes to individual goods the largest percentage change in consumption, in scenario C100, occurs in 'other travel'. The main reason for this result is that 'other travel' can be characterised as a luxury good, i.e., the income elasticity for 'other travel' is greater than 1. This means that a drop in real income will induce a decrease in the expenditures on 'other travel' which is greater, in percentage, than the drop in income. A comparison with scenario C100VAT reveals that the income effect has vanished since the recycling of tax revenues has left real income almost unchanged. The most interesting commodity, from an environmental point of view, is petroleum. Here we see that petroleum consumption will fall by approximately 2 per cent in C100, and only 0.3 per cent in C100VAT. The big difference between the two scenarios in this case reveals that the income effect is relatively important compared to the price effect. One obvious implication of this result is that taxes on petroleum are distinguished from a fiscal point of view, i.e., taxes can be raised without altering consumer behaviour in any considerable way. Another implication, however, is that ambitious environmental targets calls for very high taxes. That consumption of oil is almost unchanged, in spite of a relatively elastic demand, can also be explained by the income effects. Earlier we characterized oil as an inferior good, which means that lower income leads to higher consumption of oil.

In Figure 7.1 we illustrate the effects on petroleum consumption and welfare for a continuum of tax changes without any tax replacement. On the horizontal axes we have the percentage change in the CO_2 tax, and on the left vertical axes we measure the welfare loss in terms of dead weight loss per capita.[6] The right vertical axes measures petroleum consumption as an index, where 100 is base year consumption.

Scenario C100 is represented in Figure 7.1 by the dashed vertical line. Here we see that C100 will cause a welfare cost of approximately 250 SEK per capita and year.[7] Suppose that the objective of the policy is to reduce emissions by 6 per cent. From Figure 7.1 we see that a 270 per cent tax increase will suffice. It can also be seen that this cannot be done for free. The welfare cost in monetary terms is, according to Figure 7.1, approximately 730 SEK ($\approx$USD 100) per capita and year. It should be stressed that Figure 7.1 should be treated with care since tax rates beyond 100 per cent give rise to

---

6 The welfare effect per capita is calculated as the compensation variation (CV) minus the change in tax revenues, divided by the population.

7 This amounts to approximately 30 USD. It should be stressed that this figure does not include the tax payment.

petroleum prices far above whatever we have observed. The model might approximate petroleum consumption quite well within reasonable tax rates. However, as we move to very high tax rates it is hard to believe that the estimated relationships will still hold true.

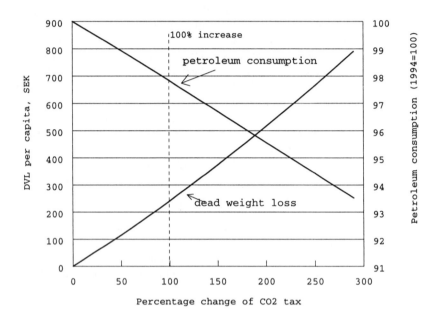

Figure 7.1   Simulation of CO_2 tax changes - effects on petroleum consumption and welfare

7.3.3   Agriculture

The environmental charge on nitrogen fertilizers was introduced in 1984 for the purpose of mitigating health and environmental problems. The charge incomes have been used to finance research and advice for reducing the use of chemicals within the agricultural sector. The environmental charge has been raised three times and amounts in 1994 to SEK 0.6/kg N, which corresponds to almost 10 per cent of the price. In the following we will investigate the options of obtaining fiscal incomes and environmental improvements from further increases in the nitrogen fertilizer tax. This requires at least two types of information: (i) the farmers' output and input adjustments to increased nitrogen fertilizers prices, and (ii) the associated nitrogen leaching and environmental damage in monetary terms. The farmers' adjustments are, like in the preceding section on partial equilibrium of the industrial sector, predicted by means of estimated input demand functions. Admittedly, it is much less trivial to obtain environmental impacts in monetary terms. Before presenting these two types of estimates we give a brief background of nitrogen fertilizer use and environmental damage. Unless otherwise stated, all data and results referred to here are found in Gren (1996).

Environmental damages and nitrogen use

In principle there are two classes of water quality problems associated with nitrogen fertilizers: high concentrations of nitrate in ground water and damages from eutrophication in coastal and marine waters. High concentrations of nitrate may cause illness for livestock and also create oxygen deficits in the blood of infants. Eutrophication implies increases in algae bloom and also changes the composition of different alga species. The first impact can create oxygen deficits at sea bottoms while the latter can generate toxic blue green algae. In this study we will only consider the damages from eutrophication simply because we have estimates of people's willingness to pay for avoiding eutrophication damages.

The environmental damages, as well as yield on arable land, are highly dependent on climatic, hydrological, and soil quality factors. It is therefore quite likely that both farmers' adjustments and environmental impacts will differ between regions in such an elongated country as Sweden with different climate zones and soil conditions. One of the first issues to solve when estimating fiscal incomes and environmental damages from nitrogen fertilizers taxes is how then to divide Sweden into different regions which satisfies the need of data for estimating input demand functions and environmental benefits. Usually, data necessary for estimating input demand functions are available on county level while data on nitrogen leaching and transports are obtained at different drainage basin levels. By means of geographical information systems data it was possible to divide the counties into seven different regions which coincide with the largest Swedish drainage basins to the Baltic Sea. In Table 7.5, we present the size of these regions and their use of nitrogen fertilizers.

Table 7.5   Total area, arable land, and nitrogen fertilizers in 1993

Region	Area in square km, total arable land		Nitrogen, tons
Bothnian Bay	116,388	522	2,394
Bothnian Sea	172,835	3,660	12,563
Mälar region	21,206	4,466	30,092
Baltic proper	62,597	8,499	65,687
The Sound	2,412	1,426	22,173
Kattegat	67,019	8,622	49,063
Skagerack	6,252	629	3,588
Total	448,709	27,824	185,520

The two northern regions - Bothnian Bay and Bothnian Sea - are big in area but relatively small with regard to the use of nitrogen fertilizers. The two southern regions Baltic Proper and Kattegat with less than half of the size of the two northern drainage basins account together for about 60 per cent of the total nitrogen use. Both fiscal incomes and environmental benefits will probably therefore depend on the farmers' adjustments and associated changes in nitrogen transport in these regions.

Nitrogen demand regressions

Like the partial equilibrium adjustments of industry and consumers, farmers' reactions to increases in the nitrogen fertilizer tax are calculated by means of an estimated nitrogen demand function. In each region, h, the representative farmer is then assumed to maximize short run profits in exactly the same way as written in (7.1), with the difference that sector i is replaced with region h. The variable production factors included in the regression are nitrogen fertilizers, N, labour, l, and the fixed factors are manure nitrogen, M, and the area of arable land, A.

$$N^h = N^h(p_y, \ p_N, \ p_l, \ M^h, \ A^h) \tag{7.13}$$

We would expect that the (weighted) output price has a positive impact on nitrogen demand, the own price effect is negative, and the other are indeterminate. The signs of p_l and M depend on labour and manure nitrogen respectively and are complements or substitutes to nitrogen fertilizers. A positive sign of A^h indicates that more nitrogen is used as the area of arable land increases. A negative sign can be interpreted as a higher intensity, nitrogen application per unit of land, when the land area decreases.

The SURE (seemingly unrelated regressions) method is used for estimating the nitrogen demand function with data for the period 1963-93 for the seven regions. The best results with respect to significance and explanatory power are the linear specification, which are presented in Table 7.6.

The nitrogen price coefficient has the expected sign for all regions and is also significant at the 5 per cent level in five of the regions. During the estimation period, there has been a steady increase in real wages and decreases in real output prices, which may explain the sign of the coefficients of these two variables.

Table 7.6   Results from nitrogen demand regressions

Region	Const.	P_N	P_y	P_l	M	A	R^2adj.
Bothnian Bay	1266	-5.95	-89.5	.93	.47	.03	0.52
t-stat.	.73	-1.18	-3.11	1.92	1.19	1.82	
Bothnian Sea	13942	-54.5	-233.9	5.27	.37	.06	0.69
t-stat.	1.91	-2.63	-1.94	2.47	.54	.84	
Mälar region	-1612	-96.05	-708.9	7.57	-1.42	0.16	0.86
t-stat	(-.12)	(-2.99)	(-3.90)	(2.43)	(-1.31)	(8.44)	
Baltic Proper	91786	-188.5	-1092.2	2.76	0.18	0.034	0.81
t-stat.	3.73	-4.42	-6.14	0.77	1.01	1.22	
the Sound*	-24807	-421.5		99.0	-3.89	.33	0.72
t-stat.	-1.54	-.69		2.67	-4.17	4.09	
Kattegat	54828	-119.3	-1174	3.69	-.01	.06	0.79
t-stat.	3.16	-2.64	-7.67	1.77	-.02	2.51	
Skagerack	5921	-32.2	-117.2	.28	-.25	.11	0.82
t-stat	3.59	-7.69	-5.20	0.70	-0.40	3.43	

* For the Sound region the general specification give poor estimates. The input prices divided by the output price generates a better fit for the Sound.

Environmental benefits and fiscal incomes

The environmental benefit estimates require information on the fertilizer nitrogen leaching and transport to the coast and associated impacts measured in monetary terms. The load to the coast from a certain deposition of nitrogen fertilizers is thus determined by the leaching at the site of deposition and the transformation of nitrogen during the transport to the coast. Unfortunately there is not enough data to cover the regions in a satisfactory way. It has therefore been necessary to assume a simple, region specific, linear relation between nitrogen fertilizers deposition and load into coastal waters.

Given these loads, the benefits estimates carried out in Söderqvist (1996) have been applied for translating these loads into monetary terms. In Söderqvist a contingent valuation study of the Baltic Sea was carried out where the scenario presented to the respondents was a Baltic Sea recovered to its 'healthy' state which prevailed prior to the 1950s. The respondents then stated their willingness to pay for a change from current conditions to the healthy state. A similar study was carried out in Poland. An overall value of the recovery of the Baltic Sea was then obtained by transferring the results from the Polish study to people in Estonia, Latvia, Lithuania, and the Russian drainage basins Kaliningrad and St. Petersburg. The Swedish results were transferred to the population of Finland, Denmark, and Germany. This gives a total estimate of an annual willingness to pay of about 31 000 million SEK. When relating this to nitrogen fertilizers, we simply assume a linear relation between the benefits and the required total nitrogen reduction necessary (545 000 tons of N) to obtain the healthy state. Needless to say, this implies very strong simplifications.

However, whether or not any environmental benefits occur at all depends on whether or not nitrogen is the limiting nutrient for biological production in the coastal and marine waters. It is regarded that all basins except for Bothnian Bay are nitrogen limited. Considering this, the calculated benefits as related to reduction in nitrogen fertilizers are presented in Table 7.7 together with the nitrogen price elasticities evaluated at the 1993 values of the variables.

Table 7.7   Environmental benefits per kg nitrogen reduction and nitrogen price elasticities

	Bothn Bay	Bothn. Sea	Mälar region	Baltic Proper	The Sound	Katte- gatt	Skage- rack
Environmental benefit	0	11	2	4	12	6	10
Price elasticity	0.27	0.45	0.34	0.32	0.12	0.25	0.51

Given that we are interested in low erosion of the tax base and high environmental benefits, we would welcome that low nitrogen price elasticities occur in regions with high unit environmental benefits. A low nitrogen price elasticity implies a small decrease in nitrogen use, and, hence, relatively high fiscal incomes. This seems to apply very well for the Sound region, which has the lowest price elasticity and the highest unit environmental benefit. On the other hand, this region accounts only for a small share of total use of nitrogen fertilizers.

In Figure 7.2, results are presented for calculations of fiscal revenues and environmental benefits for different nitrogen fertilizer taxes measured as increases in the 1994 fertilizer nitrogen price.

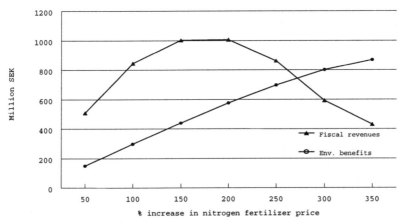

Figure 7.2   Fiscal incomes and environmental benefits from taxes on nitrogen fertilizer price

The simulation results in Figure 7.2 indicate a relatively robust tax base, where the fiscal incomes start to decrease first at tax levels exceeding a 200 per cent increase in the nitrogen fertilizer price. This is explained by the relatively low price elasticities in all regions. The estimated environmental benefits show a steady increase until taxes higher than 300 per cent of the price.

7.4   CONCLUDING REMARKS

The objective of this paper is to give a brief historical view of the development of environmental policy in Sweden, with some emphasis on use of economic instruments. Another objective is to give an analysis of the impacts from the Swedish CO_2 tax and the tax on nitrogen in fertilizers.

To conclude we have shown that environmental policy has a long history in Sweden. Economic instruments, such as taxes and subsidies, are however a quite recent phenomenon. One can say that the use of economic instruments started in the seventies with the subsidies to municipal waste water treatment plants. Environmental taxes were brought into focus with the Commission on Environmental Charges, which delivered its final report in 1990. The general tax reform in 1990 and 1991 was another milestone in Swedish environmental policy. In conjunction with the tax reform, a tax on the carbon content in fuels, the CO_2 tax, was introduced, as well as the sulphur tax. The analysis of the CO_2 tax shows that the tax has the intended effect in the sense that it tends to reduce emissions. However, it is also shown that effects from further increases of carbon taxes probably have moderate effect on Swedish emissions, at least in the short run. This should be seen in light of the fact that the use of fossil fuels in Sweden has been considerably reduced during the last 20 years.

The analysis presented here should be viewed as a short run analysis. Concerning the industry it is assumed that capital stocks are fixed, which means that the long run effects due to capital adjustments are ignored. The results concerning household behaviour should also be regarded as short run results. The reason is that the data used only includes consumption of non-durable goods, which means that a price change in our model only affects the consumption of non-durable goods.

The estimates of environmental benefits from taxes on nitrogen fertilizers provide one of the few, and maybe also the only, study on such a large scale as all Sweden. There are good reasons for the lack of similar studies. The main problem, although difficult enough, is not to estimate benefits from the environmental damages caused by nitrogen loads, but instead to relate these benefit estimates to nitrogen fertilizer use. It is evident from the study presented here that very simplifying assumptions are required to reach any conclusion concerning this relation between fertilizer use and environmental benefits. It is then noteworthy that this provides an area where we have a large amount of information on both nutrient transports and environmental benefits. When considering the need for making similar linkages for other pollutants we realize that we are far from being able to make appropriate predictions of environmental benefits from taxes on pollutant emissions.

REFERENCES

Bovenberg, A.L. and Goulder, L.H. (1996), 'Optimal Environmental Taxation in the Presence of Other Taxes: General Equilibrium Analyses', *American Economic Review* **86**, 1996.

Dargay, J. (1983), 'The Demand for Energy in Swedish Manufacturing, in *Energy in Swedish Manufacturing*, IUI Stockholm.

Deaton and Muellbauer (1980a), 'An Almost Ideal Demand System', *American Economic Review* **70**, 312-26.

Franzén, M. (1994), *Gasoline Demand - A Comparison of Models*, Ekonomiska studier nr. 49, Handelshögskolan vid Göteborgs Universitet.

Franzén, M. and Sterner, T. (1990), *The Demand for Gasoline i the OECD*, Memorandum No. 135, Department of Economics, Gothenburg University.

Gren, I-M. (1996), 'Fiscal incomes and environmental benefits from taxes on fertilizers and pesticides', (in Swedish) in *Experts' Report to Skatteväxlingskommittén*, SOU 1996:117, Ministry of Finance, Stockholm, 167-205.

Hansson-Bruzewitz, U. (1997), 'Höjd koldioxidskatt och höjd skatt på elektrisk kraft: effekter på hushållens välfärd och konsumtion', in *Skatter, miljö och Sysselsättning, SOU 1997:11*, underlagsrapporter till Skatteväxlingskommitténs slutbetänkande.

Harrison, G. and Kriström, B. (1997), 'Carbon Taxes in Sweden', in *Skatter, miljö och Sysselsättning, SOU 1997:11*, underlagsrapporter till Skatteväxlingskommitténs slutbetänkande.

Oates, W.E. (1995), 'Green Taxes: Can We Protect the Environment and Improve the Tax System at the Same Time?', *Southern Economic Journal* **61**, 1995.

SOU 1989:21. *Sätt värde på miljön. Miljöavgifter på svavel och klor.* Delbetänkande från miljöavgiftsutredningen. Allmänna förlaget, Stockholm 1989.

SOU 1989:83. *Ekonomiska styrmedel i miljöpolitiken.* Delbetänkande från miljöavgiftsutredningen. Allmänna förlaget, Stockholm 1989.

SOU 1990:59. *Sätt värde på miljön. Miljöavgifter och andra ekonomiska styrmedel.* Slutbetänkande från miljöavgiftsutredningen. Allmänna förlaget, Stockholm 1990.

SOU 1997:11. *Skatter, miljö och sysselsättning*, Slutbetänkande från Skatteväxlingskommittén. Fritzes, Stockholm 1997.

SOU 1997:11 *Skatter, miljö och sysselsättning*, Underlagsrappporter från Skatteväxlingskommittén. Fritzes, Stockholm 1997.

Sterner, T. och Dahl, C. (1991*)*, 'Gasoline Demand Modelling: Theory and Application' in Sterner, T. (ed), *International Energy Modelling*, Chapman and Hall, London.

Söderqvist, T. (1996), 'Contingent valuation of a less eutrophicated Baltic Sea', Beijer Discussion Papers Series No. 88, Beijer Institute, Stockholm.

Walfridsson, B. och Hjalmarsson, L. (1991*)*, *Kapitalbildning, Kapitalutnyttjande och Produktivitet.* Expertrapport nr. 3 till Produktivitetsdelegationen, Allmänna Förlaget, Stockholm.

8. Taxes and Labour Supply in Sweden - A Meta Analysis[*]

Magnus Wikström

8.1 INTRODUCTION

Changes in environmental taxation with the purpose of increasing environmental quality have during the last few years been coupled with changes in traditional labour market related taxes. The idea with such policy changes would be to lessen distortions due to environmental damage and at the same time reduce distortions in the labour market. Early work viewed tax swaps as successful (Oates (1991)), thus indicating that a free lunch may be available. Based on general equilibrium analyses, a number of authors have later identified several mechanisms that lead to qualified statements concerning the correctness of the free lunch argument (Bovenberg and de Mooij (1994), Bovenberg and van der Ploeg (1994) and Goulder (1994)). The free lunch argument of 'tax swap reform' is often seen as dependent on effects such as substitutability between 'dirty' goods and leisure, something we know very little about. The success of an environmental tax reform also depends on the effects of taxation on the labour market *per se*. One important piece of information, therefore, concerns the effects of different labour market taxes on the allocation of hours of work and employment.

In this chapter, I will add to the big jigsaw puzzle that comprises the effects of tax swaps on the economy. The purpose is twofold. First, I will discuss the present state of knowledge regarding the effects of income taxation on labour supply in Sweden. Second, I will take the analysis a little further by conducting a meta-analysis on a number of Swedish labour supply studies in order to explain differences in results among them. The chapter is organized as follows. Section 2 discusses empirical results in the form of labour supply elasticities from 11 different labour supply studies using Swedish data. We conclude that the qualitative results indicate that labour supply curves are positively sloped functions of wages and negatively

[*] I would like to thank Larry Goulder, Karl-Gustaf Löfgren and Åsa Rosén for valuable comments.

dependent on non labour income components. There are, however, quite large quantitative differences among the studies. Section 3 first proposes a number of explanations for the differences among studies and then performs regressions to explain these differences. The conclusion from the exercise is that a large part of the variation in the data can be explained with relatively simple means. In particular, the estimated elasticities appear to be influenced by what kind of data set and sample selection criteria that have been used. Finally, Section 4 concludes the chapter.

8.2 TAXES AND LABOUR SUPPLY IN SWEDEN

8.2.1 Empirical labour supply estimates in Sweden

The decision to supply labour have frequently been subject to empirical analysis in Sweden. There are probably several causes for the relatively large number of studies that have been conducted in Sweden during the last decade or so. Around 1980, the Swedish income tax system was highly progressive with marginal tax rates of up to 80 per cent or more. At the time, a number of economists and politicians had expressed concern over the adverse effects on economic behaviour a strongly progressive tax system may have.[1] A few early contributions emerged that shed light on these issues (e.g. Blomquist (1983) and Jacobsson 1982)). During the 80s, increased awareness of the problems of highly progressive tax systems lead to changes in the tax system. For example, in 1984 the maximum marginal tax rate in the national income taxation was 52 per cent and the number of marginal tax rates was 18. By 1988, the number of marginal tax rates in the national income taxation had decreased to four and the maximum (national) marginal tax rate was 45 per cent.[2] As a part of the government intentions to simplify the income tax system, continued interest was devoted to labour supply issues. A third wave of empirical labour supply studies were initiated either as a consequence of the Swedish tax reform of 1990, or simply from continued interest among researchers in the issues concerning labour supply and taxation.

Thus, there is a large number of studies that can be used to shed light on the effects of taxation on labour supply. In this section, I will present results from 11 different labour supply studies using Swedish data.[3] The studies all

---

1   See, for example, Myrdahl (1977).
2   In addition, local governments levy income taxes that are, in principle, proportional. The average local tax rate was approximately 30 per cent during the second half of the 80s, meaning that the maximum of the total marginal income tax rate was above 75 per cent.
3   The studies are Aaberge et al. (1989), Ackum-Agell and Apel (1993), Andersson (1989), Aronsson and Karlsson (1995), Aronsson and Palme (1995), Aronsson and Wikström (1994), Blomquist (1983), Blomquist and Hansson-Brusewitz (1990), Flood and MaCurdy (1992), Jacobsson (1982), and Sacklén (1995).

have in common that they use cross-sectional data to estimate wage and income effects. The selection made is not complete, but should be fairly representative for the Swedish labour supply literature.[4] The studies report estimates of a total of 38 labour supply equations, 24 male supply equations and 14 female equations.[5] The distribution of equations between males and females is most likely to be a result of the belief that male labour supply is easier to study, probably as a consequence of the higher labour force participation rates among men. Figures 8.1 and 8.2 display wage and income elasticities for the selected studies.

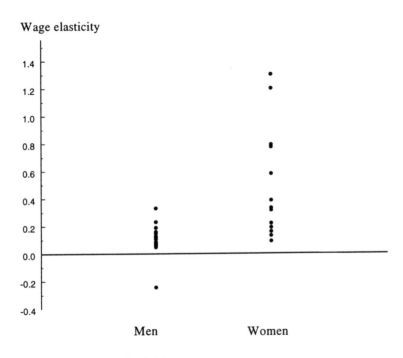

Figure 8.1   Wage elasticities

One central theme emerging is that male hours of work appear to react only little to changes in wages. As is evident from Figure 8.1, the wage elasticity is

---

4   Other reviews of the Swedish labour supply literature are Aronsson and Walker (1995) and Löfgren (1990). Killingsworth (1988) contains a review of the international literature.

5   The reader should note that this survey does not attempt to study the statistical significance of various estimates. The main reason is that confidence bands are not possible to calculate for many of the studies. In addition to providing information about the robustness of results, t-statistics and the like can be used to test hypotheses of specification searches.

Income elasticity

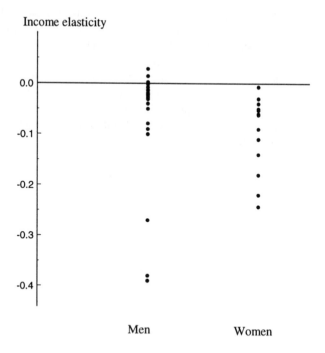

Figure 8.2   Income elasticities

generally positive and the dispersion among the studies are modest. The
median of elasticities in the sample is approximately 0.08. Female elasticities
are generally larger with a median of about 0.3. Figure 8.1 also shows that the
dispersion is larger for female as compared to male wage elasticities. Turning
to income elasticities, the usual assumption is that income components
decrease hours of work at a given net wage, i.e. leisure is assumed to be a
normal good. Although some studies have found positive elasticities for men,
the tendency here is that leisure may be interpreted as a normal good. The
majority of male studies give elasticities of -0.05 or larger, indicating a
relative insensitivity of hours of work to changes in (unearned) income. The
median income elasticity is -0.06 for women and -0.02 for men. These results
concerning wage and income elasticities support the hypothesis of the male as
the main income earner of the family, where taxation is expected to have
larger effects on females than males.

When it comes to the effects of taxes on labour supply, interest is usually
devoted to the compensated wage elasticities. Tax reforms tends to be
financed, which means that changes in the income tax system are generally
accompanied by some other change so as to balance the government budget.
One simple case of comparison is to redistribute the tax revenue in a lump

sum manner to the working population, and this can be illustrated (although not perfectly) by the compensated elasticities. Compensated elasticities also serve as a base for calculating the excess burden of taxation, and as a check of the validity of the theoretical model. Symmetry and negative definiteness of the Slutsky matrix is the simple one good case equivalent to a positive compensated wage effect. In the present sample, compensated elasticities have been calculated for 26 of the 38 equations, out of which 10 are female labour supply equations. Figure 8.3 shows compensated elasticities for male and female labour supply equations.

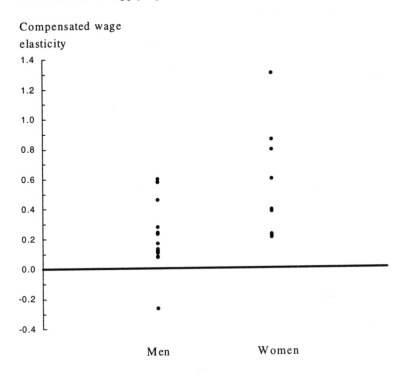

Figure 8.3   Compensated wage elasticities

Figure 8.3 underscores the view that females respond more to changes in the tax system. Note that the compensated elasticity is negative in one case only. This means that it is not generally possible to dismiss the simple labour supply model on grounds of theoretical inconsistencies when estimated on cross-sectional data. Based on the sample of studies used in the present analysis, therefore, it seems as if income taxes do have a negative impact on hours of work.

8.3 EXPLAINING DIFFERENCES AMONG LABOUR SUPPLY STUDIES

8.3.1 Hypotheses regarding differences among the studies

Although the conclusions regarding the qualitative effects of tax reform appear to be straightforward, the vast quantitative differences among the studies and among men and women deserves further attention. This section therefore takes into account a number of differences among the studies in order to study whether the differences in elasticities can be explained or not.

A first difference concerns the *choice of data*. In Sweden, three different data sets have been used to study the determinants of hours of work. Most frequently, the Swedish level of living survey (LNU) has been used. A couple of studies use the so called HUS data (the Swedish Household Market and Nonmarket Activities Survey), and another two use Statistics Sweden's Household Income Survey (HINK). Hypotheses regarding the impact of differences in data are most frequently directed towards issues of measurement of hours of work, wages and non labour income. In addition, surveys tend to differ when it comes to the number of background variables available. For example, the LNU-survey asks direct questions about hours of work and hourly wages, while the HINK-survey calculates wages on the basis of hours of work and labour income. If hours of work are subject to measurement errors, wages will generally be influenced by these errors if they are calculated as in the HINK-survey. In particular, we would expect to introduce a negative correlation between wages and hours of work. This will, therefore, give a tendency for a backward bending labour supply curve relative to the 'true' supply curve, and will give lower wage elasticities compared with data based on measurement of all the components of labour income. In the LNU survey, on the other hand, wages are probably reported with measurement error. This may also give rise to biases depending upon the exact form of the measurement error.

Another difference between studies is *sample selection*. Most studies use prime aged persons to study the determinants of hours of work. Prime aged persons are those aged 25 to 55 years. The main reason for selecting the sample in this way is the belief that persons that are close to entry or exit in the labour market behave differently than persons in the middle of their working lives. In particular, if possibilities of education and retirement are present, we would expect those persons to be more sensitive in their choice of hours of work to changes in the hourly wage and non labour income.

Methodological differences are pronounced in the labour supply literature. Usually, income tax systems are progressive in nature, and in practice they are piecewise linear. The variations in quantitative results may reflect the difficult statistical problems created by piecewise linear budget constraints.[6] Several different methods to take into account tax progressivity have been proposed. An early way to estimate labour supply functions when the tax system is progressive was to use information only stemming from the tax segment where the individual had it's observed number of hours. This so called linearisation method will generally give rise to biased estimates if hours of work are measured with error, since large errors cause the observed marginal wage and virtual income component to differ from the values that are optimal from the viewpoint of the individual. In the case of progressive taxation, this method will give a tendency towards a negative bias in the measurement of the wage effect and a positive bias in the measurement of the (virtual) income effect.[7] The problem here is one of endogeneity of the wage and virtual income variables. In order to correct for the endogeneity problem, two step estimation methods have been proposed. A different approach, the so called Hausman method, is to take the whole budget constraint into account in the estimation and perform the estimation using a maximum likelihood technique. By explicitly modelling the choice set and taking the information into account in the estimation routine, the endogeneity problem is accounted for.

Both these methods have been criticized in the labour supply literature, and the issue does not appear to be fully resolved.[8] According to the so called MaCurdy critique, the Hausman method imposes constraints on the parameter values, and these constraints are, in principle, claimed to resemble non-negative compensated wage effects. On the other hand, instrumental variable approaches give estimates that are often argued to be sensitive to the choice of the instrument set. This may have (at least) two effects. First, instrumental variable methods should give larger differences among studies if researchers tend to use different instrument sets. Second, the endogeneity problems might not be fully resolved if the instruments used are poor, and thus the original bias remains.[9] Another issue concerns the small sample properties of different estimators. Blomquist (1996) performs a Monte Carlo experiment to highlight this issue. Blomquist's study has some interesting implications. For example, there does not seem to be one best estimation method. Rather, the proper estimation method is 'situation specific'. In particular, biases depend on the nature of measurement errors and the size of the sample in use. This suggests

---

6   See Moffitt (1990) for a non technical treatment of the econometrics of piecewise linear budget constraints.

7   The term virtual income refers to the intercept income (at zero hours) that results from 'linearising' the budget constraint around the observe choice.

8   See MaCurdy et al. (1990) and Blomquist (1995) for different views regarding the problems of the Hausman method.

9   A third point is perhaps that, in comparison to the Hausman method, instrumental variable methods are relatively inexpensive to use in terms of computer time. This also means that the 'cost' of engaging in specification searches are larger when the Hausman method is used.

that there may be interaction effects between the use of data and estimation method when it comes to explaining differences in elasticities among labour supply studies.

A fourth difference between the studies concerns the *mathematical form* used. A small majority of the studies use simple linear or loglinear forms to estimate labour supply responses. The rest use more flexible forms where the marginal wage and virtual income may have positive as well as negative effects on hours of work. It is not clear, *a priori*, if more flexible forms will give rise to different supply elasticities. Linear supply curves impose restrictions on the data, for example that the supply curve is always a positively or negatively sloped function of the wage. While this may be important for predicting individual behaviour, restrictions to linear specifications may not be important at all when it comes to predicting 'average' behavioural responses.

Yet another difference concerns issues of *family labour supply*. Some studies have had the ambitious purpose of simultaneously estimating male and female labour supply curves referring to household or family labour supply models. In these studies, a number of additional effects are allowed for. For example cross-wage effects may be studied and a richer set of hypotheses regarding the maximizing framework can be tested. Finally, it is commonly observed that male hours of work are concentrated around 1 800 to 2 100 hours a year. Simple labour supply models cannot easily account for this fact. Therefore, some studies try to take into account the possibility that hours of work are delimited by circumstances outside the individuals control by modelling explicitly that individuals may be rationed, so called *quantity constraints*.

8.3.2 Estimation results - elasticity equations

With the purpose of examining of how the above factors influence the estimated elasticities, six different dummy variables are constructed. To take into account the differences in data, a variable denoted LNU is constructed. The variable takes the value one if the equation is performed using data from the Level of Living Survey and zero otherwise. In a similar spirit, the variable PRIME is a dummy indicating if the sample selected is of age 25 to 55. The differences in method among the studies is measured using the Hausman method as the reference case. So, the dummy LINMETHOD takes the value one for the equations that in one way or another use a method where the information about the budget set is limited to the segment where the individual's hours of work are observed. The dummy FAMILY takes the value one if male and female hours of work are estimated simultaneously, and FLEXIBLE controls for those equations that have a flexible form. Finally, RATIONED takes the value one if the equation explicitly models labour supply as a choice potentially subject to quantity constraints. Table A1 in the Appendix show descriptive statistics for the variables used.

With respect to the relatively few degrees of freedom available, the following estimation strategy is used. To start with, I use a general specification including all six dummy variables. The dummy with the lowest t-value is dropped, conditional on that it is below one in absolute value. The procedure is then repeated until no dummy variable with a t-value below one remains. The estimates of the elasticity equations for males and females are given in Table 8.1.

One emerging theme from this exercise, is the importance of the sample selection. The variable PRIME is significantly determined (on the five per cent level of significance) in all elasticity equations except for the female income elasticity equation. Thus, it appears as if prime aged individuals respond less to changes in the tax system. One factor that appears to explain differences in the female equations is the data. LNU is positive indicating that using data from the Level of Living Survey gives higher elasticities

Table 8.1   Elasticity equations

Variable	Men			Women		
	Wage	Income	Comp.	Wage	Income	Comp.
CONSTANT	0.25	-0.29	0.59	0.32	-0.21	0.34
	(3.8)	(-7.6)	(6.7)	(2.2)	(-6.9)	(4.1)
LNU	0.05	0.07	-	1.35	0.10	0.96
	(1.0)	(1.5)		(4.4)	(1.8)	(6.1)
PRIME	-0.21	0.18	-0.50	-0.84	-0.08	-0.53
	(-3.1)	(3.5)	(-5.2)	(-2.8)	(-1.4)	(-3.2)
LINMETHOD	-0.05	-	-	-0.15	0.12	-0.15
	(-1.1)			(-1.1)	(4.1)	(-1.6)
FAMILY	-0.07	-	-0.23	-0.19	0.05	-
	(-1.1)		(-2.1)	(-1.1)	(1.5)	
RATIONED	-	-	-	0.28	-	-
				(1.1)		
FLEXIBLE	-	0.06	-	-0.18	0.04	-
		(1.5)		(-1.1)	(1.4)	
R^2	0.40	0.66	0.72	0.83	0.75	0.91
F-test	3.11	13.20	16.67	5.56	4.70	20.24
Number of observations	24	24	16	14	14	10

Note: t-values are given within parentheses.

throughout. At least when compared to the HINK data, this is expected since the latter survey uses hours information to construct the wage measure. Therefore, it supports the hypothesis that using hours information to construct the wage measure may alter the estimates of the underlying preferences. On the other hand, no strong effects can be found in the male equations.

There results concerning the method used are interesting although not conclusive. If linearisation methods give rise to bias (because of endogeneity problems), these effects should show up in the wage and income elasticity equations, but not necessarily in the compensated elasticity equations. The direction of the bias of using insufficient instruments is that the wage effect is underestimated and the income effect overestimated.[10] If the MaCurdy critique is correct, the important effect should be in the compensated elasticity equations, but it will also influence the wage and/or income elasticities. In this case the wage effect would be overestimated and/or the income effect underestimated. In the present study, I cannot draw conclusions regarding the correctness of the two approaches, but only if the results differ between the approaches. There are no important effects in the male equations, meaning that I can reject the hypothesis that the LINMETHOD dummy significantly affects the elasticities. However, there is a tendency for the wage elasticity to be lower when using a linearisation method. Among the female equations, the effect is significantly determined in the income elasticity equation only. There is also a tendency for the wage elasticity and the compensated wage elasticity to be lower when using a linearisation method. Therefore, there is weak evidence suggesting that the results depend on the method used. A more thorough analysis, including additional studies where differences in methods when it comes to analysing differences in instrument sets, sample sizes and so on, would perhaps be time well spent.[11]

We also conclude that FAMILY significantly contributes to the compensated elasticities of males, but do not appear to have any other effect. In simultaneous models, cross wage effects are often found to be insignificantly determined, and so one interpretation is that these effects are zero.[12] The other two potential explanations, measured by RATIONED and FLEXIBLE do not appear to have any important effects. It may seem a bit surprising that studies that try to take quantity constraints into account do not

10 The original bias, stemming from neglecting the endogeneity of the wage and income measures and performing the estimation by the use of OLS, may be severe. Blomquist (1996) conducts a Monte Carlo experiment. He finds that the bias is large even when measurement errors are reasonably small.

11 I have also tried specifications where LNU is interacted with LINMETHOD. This does not add anything important in explaining the variation in the data.

12 In a somewhat different vein, however, Aronsson (1994) rejects weak separability of male hours in a study of married womens labour supply. This indicates that cross wage effects may be important. One explanation for the vast differences among studies concerning cross wage effects may be problems of identification due to multicollinearity.

report elasticities different from other studies. Comparisons within these studies also confirm the results here. The explanation here is probably that most individuals report that they are quite happy with their present number of hours worked in the market, and the contribution of modelling quantity constraints will consequently be small.[13] Finally, we note that all six regressions are significant as measured by conventional F-tests.

8.4 CONCLUSIONS AND SUGGESTIONS FOR FUTURE WORK

Labour supply models have frequently been applied to Swedish data. Most studies find that compensated wage elasticities are positive, indicating that it is difficult to reject underlying maximization hypotheses. The studies differ when it comes to the quantitative estimates of labour supply elasticities. Male elasticities are typically found to be more modest than female elasticities, and the dispersion among studies is larger for females. In this chapter, I have incorporated some of the observable differences in order to study if it is possible to explain differences in wage and income elasticities. I identify six factors that may help in explaining these differences. The use of data set and sample selection appear to be the most important differences. Interestingly, I also find weak evidence for the hypothesis that differences in the results depend on the statistical method used to estimate labour supply responses. In all, the regressions explain between 40 and 90 per cent of the variation in the data. The fact that supply elasticities, at least when it comes to male labour supply, appear to be small in magnitude suggest that taxation does not much affect labour supply. However, it is a somewhat different matter what effects taxation do have on welfare. Income tax may have rather serious effects on welfare anyway, since the welfare effects also depend on the size of the wedge between net and gross wages.[14]

The relative richness of empirical labour supply studies appear to imply that this is a good area to conduct meta analyses. A number of questions may successfully be answered using this approach. Let me take a few examples. First, meta analyses may shed new light on methodological controversies. Second, cross country differences may be analysed using this approach. It appears as if American and British studies more often give negative wage elasticities compared to Swedish studies.[15] The reasons for this are, however,

---

13 See the studies by Aronsson and Karlsson (1995) and Sacklén (1995).

14 A few studies have tried to estimate the size of the welfare losses due to taxation (see e.g. Blomquist (1983) and Aronsson and Palme (1995)), and generally supports the idea that income taxes have substantial welfare effects even though the effects on labour supply are rather modest.

15 See, for example, the studies referred to in Killingsworth (1988).

not clear. Finally, more controversial questions such as the researchers influence on empirical results may also be addressed. After all, taxation has an important political dimension and the views expressed by researchers may partly reflect their prior beliefs.

APPENDIX

Table 8.A1 Descriptive statistics

Variable	Men		Women	
	Mean	Std dev	Mean	Std dev
Wage elasticity	0.10	0.10	0.47	0.40
Income elasticity	-0.08	0.13	-0.10	0.07
Compensated elasticity	0.22	0.22	0.52	0.38
LNU	0.67	-	0.50	-
PRIME	0.75	-	0.43	-
LINMETHOD	0.29	-	0.43	-
FAMILY	0.21	-	0.36	-
FLEXIBLE	0.33	-	0.43	-
RATIONED	0.42	-	0.14	-

Note: The number of observations (equations) are 24 for men and 16 for women. Descriptives for the compensated elasticities are calculated on the basis of 16 observations for men and 10 for women.

REFERENCES

Aaberge R., Ström, S. and Wennemo, T. (1989), 'Skatt, arbeidstilbud och intektsfordelning i Sverige', *Bilaga 2 till SOU 1989:33 Reformerad inkomstbeskattning*.

Ackum-Agell, S. and Apel, M. (1993), 'Female Labour Supply and Taxes in Sweden - A Comparison of Estimation Approaches', in S. Ackum-Agell (ed.), *Essays on Work and Pay* (dissertation), Economic Studies 15, Uppsala universitet.

Aronsson, T. (1994), 'A Simple Test for Weak Separability between Male and Female Labour Supply', *Umeå Economic Studies* no. **328**.

Aronsson, T. and Karlsson, N. (1995), 'Taxes and Quantity Constraints in Model of Male Labour Supply in Sweden', mimeo.

Aronsson, T. and Palme, M. (1995), 'A Decade of Tax and Benefit Reforms in Sweden - Effects on Labour Supply, Welfare and Inequality', mimeo, forthcoming in *Economica*.

Aronsson, T. and Walker, J.R. (1995), 'The Effects of Sweden's Welfare State on Labor Supply Incentives', *SNS Occational Paper* **64**.

Aronsson, T. and Wikström, M. (1994), 'Nonlinear Taxes in a Life-Cycle Consistent Model of Family Labour Supply', *Empirical Economics* **19**, 1-17, 717-18.

Blomquist, N.S. (1983), 'The Effect of Income Taxation on the Labour Supply of Married Men in Sweden', *Journal of Public Economics* **22**, 169-97.

Blomquist, S. (1995), 'Restrictions in Labor Supply Estimation: Is the MaCurdy Critique Correct?', *Economics Letters* **47**.

Blomquist, S. (1996), 'Estimation Methods for Male Labor Supply Functions: How to Take Account of Nonlinear Taxes', *Journal of Econometrics* **70**, 383-405.

Blomquist, N.S. and Hansson-Brusewitz, U. (1990), 'The Effect of Taxes on Male and Female Labor Supply in Sweden', *Journal of Human Resources* **25**, 317-57.

Bovenberg, A.L. and de Mooij, R.A. (1994), 'Environmental Levies and Distortionary Taxation', *American Economic Review* **94**(4), 1085-9.

Bovenberg, A.L. and van der Ploeg, F. (1994a), 'Environmental Policy, Public Finance and the Labour Market in a Second-best World', *Journal of Public Economics* **55**, 349-90.

Flood, L. and MaCurdy, T. (1992), 'Work Disincentive Effects of Taxes: An Empirical Analysis of Swedish Men', mimeo, Gothenburg University.

Goulder, L. (1994), 'Environmental Taxation and the "Double Dividend" a Readers Guide', mimeo.

Jacobsson, R. (1982), 'Three Papers on Estimation of Labour Supply Responses on Swedish Data', mimeo, Umeå University.

Killingsworth, M.R. (1988), *Labor Supply*, Cambridge, Cambridge University Press (2nd edition).

Löfgren, K.G. (1990), 'Utbudet av arbetskraft och den svenska skattereformen', in J. Agell, K.G. Mäler and J. Södersten (eds.), *Ekonomiska perspektiv på skattereformen*, Ekonomiska rådet, Konjunkturinstitutet.

McCurdy, T., Green, D. and Paarsch, H. (1990), 'Assesing Empirical Approaches for Analyzing Taxes and Labor Supply', *Journal of Human Resources* **25**, 415-89.

Moffitt, R. (1990), 'The Econometrics of Kinked Budget Constraints, *Journal of Economic Perspectives* **4**, 119-39.

Myrdahl, G. (1978), 'Dags för ett nytt skattesystem!', *Ekonomisk debatt* **7**

Oates, W.E. (1991), 'Pollution Charges as a Source of Public Revenues, *Discussion Paper No.* **QE92-05**, Resources for the Future, Washington, DC.

Sacklén, H. (1995), 'Labour Supply, Income Taxes and Hours Constraints in Sweden', *Working Paper* **2**, Department of Economics, Uppsala University.

Wikström, M. (1996), 'Skatter, sysselsättning och arbetsutbud - en kunskapsöversikt', *Expertrapporter från Skatteväxlingskommittén, SOU* **117**, Fritzes, Stockholm.

Index